^{the}Afterlife

glimpses of heaven & hell

TONY EVANS

Printed in the United States of America

ISBN 1-930893-02-7

All material is taken from the teaching ministry of Dr. Tony Evans.

You can contact The Urban Alternative by phone 1-800-800-3222 or by
e-mail: info@tonyevans.org or by visiting tonyevans.org.

CONTENTS

Dr. Evans' series of six messages titled *The Afterlife: Glimpses of Heaven and Hell* is available on CD and MP3 download. For ordering information, contact The Urban Alternative at 1-800-800-3222 or by visiting tonyevans.org.

INTRODUCTION

Death is hard, funerals are tougher, but the cemetery experience maybe even worse—because often that coffin has been lowered into the earth, there is such a sense of finality.

If you're a believer in Jesus Christ, death is still hard, funerals are still tough, and the cemetery experience is still no fun. But you know that the grave is not the end. And that's not all. If your departed loved one is a Christian, then you have a reason to celebrate. Those tears may flow, but make them happy tears, because that one you loved has now gone to be with Jesus.

Many times, when Christians lose someone dear to them, they don't choose to grieve; rather, they choose to celebrate life—not only the life that has already been lived on this earth, but the new life that lies ahead for all who put their trust in God's Son.

When this happens, those in the world come to the funeral. They sit in the pew. They listen to the testimonies. They listen to the eulogy. They listen to the music. And they scratch their heads. They don't understand. The atmosphere is not that of hopelessness, despair, or utter grief that will never go away. Instead, there's hope, peace, and joy. We can experience this joy because we have embraced the message of God's Word, and because we have embraced Jesus Christ as our Savior, as our Lord, as our God.

We have been given the responsibility of helping the world understand the source of our hope. Are you capable of opening your Bible and sharing with yoru neighbor or your co-worker or your classmate what God says about life after death?

In this study, we're going to look at the information God has given us in His Word about death and the afterlife. You're going to read about a place called heaven, and you're going to read about a place called hell. And if you will prayerfully consider the words of Scripture, God will give you a glimpse of what those two places are like. Though the Bible does not tell us everything there is to know about heaven and hell, we have enough information to make a wise decision about where we want to spend eternity.

Have you examined the information for yourself and made your choice? Are you sure you made the right one? Until you have breathed your last breath, there is still time for you to change your mind.

Or maybe you're still undecided. You have heard about Jesus Christ, you have heard even more about Christians (perhaps in a bad light), and you're still not sure if becoming a Christian yourself is what you want to do.

Wherever you are, I just want you to be sure that you have made the right decision and that you are not misled about what's awaiting us on the other side of this life.

I'm going to ask you to do one thing: Read this book. Think about what you're reading. Take time to meditate on the Scriptures that you see. Decide right now that you will finish this study, and I promise you that by the time you get to the last page, you will have enough information to make a wise decision about the afterlife...or help someone else make an informed decision.

My friend, it is my prayer that as you read, the Holy Spirit will open your eyes to understand the Scriptures. May you see truth, and may God guide you in your study of the afterlife.

Tony Evans

LESSON 1

WHAT HAPPENS WHEN YOU DIE?

Now I lay...

me down to sleep. I pray the Lord my soul to keep. And if I die before I wake, I pray the Lord my soul to take.

Chances are you've heard this prayer before. It's the prayer of a child who has been taught from an early age that there is such a thing as a soul, that there is such a thing as death, and that there is such a thing as life after death.

> You can be certain that unless Christ comes first, you and I will both die. Not to think about the afterlife is to miss the inevitable, and we don't want to do that.

As we grow older and get so encumbered in the realities of time, it is so easy to forget that simple prayer ... and even easier to lose our sense of eternity.

When we were born into this world, we were born to die. Not one of us is exempt from the grave, the box, and the field. Unless Jesus Christ returns first, we are all going to die. I don't want to sound morbid, but we will not be able to understand the afterlife without first looking at death.

As a society, we try so hard to avoid the subject of death. We try to camouflage it by using fancy words like "passed on" or "family plot," but the reality is that you and I are marching toward a destiny at the local cemetery.

The question is, what's on the other side? Everybody has an opinion, but here's the problem: The people who are giving their opinions haven't been there and back.

If we want to catch a glimpse of the afterlife, then we need to hear from somebody who has been there.

1. DEATH: IS INEVITABLE

Some of you may be terrified of the thought of death. The cracking of steps at night may send you into paranoia. You may tremble in fear because of stories you have heard about the "Grim Reaper." Death may be a hard topic for you, but it's worth studying.

The odds that you will eventually die are pretty good. In fact, the Bible says they're even better: "It is appointed for men to die once and after this comes judgment" (Hebrews 9:27).

Did you catch that word *appointed?* You may be late for a lot of things in your life, but this is one date you won't miss. Nobody skips this appointment. The problem is, we're not certain when it's going to happen. It could be a sudden heart attack, a terminal disease, a head on collision, or falling asleep and not waking up.

Though the inevitability of death is certain, the *when* and *where* and *how* are uncertain. If your stomach cramps, you start wondering what's going on. If you feel gas pains, you begin to panic. If your right side starts to ache, you think, "Could this be something else?"

But, regardless of the uncertainties, you can be certain that unless Christ comes first, you and I will both die. Not to think about the afterlife is to miss the inevitable, and we don't want to do that.

A lot of people come to church for an hour or two on Sunday, but spend most of their week as if there is no death and no afterlife. In fact, they have whole systems available to help them forget that death even exists. They're only avoiding the inevitable.

Maybe you figure you'll be able to score enough points just in time to secure your spot in the clouds. That reminds me of a story. It's fictional, but it makes a good point.

One day, a man arrived at the Pearly Gates and came across Saint Peter. Good old Saint Peter said to him, "Tell me what good things you did in your lifetime." He said, "Well, uh, I, uh, I'll tell you one thing I did. There was this biker who was stealing this old woman's purse, and I saw him stealing it. So I grabbed him and threw him to the ground in order to save this woman's purse from being stolen." Saint Peter asked, "When did this happen?" He said, "About two or three minutes ago."

There are other people who think they're so important that they don't have to worry themselves with such things as the afterlife. I want to ask you a question: What is the name of one of your great-great-grandmothers? Okay. Now, what about your great-great-great-grand-mother? What was her name?

> A lot of people come to church for an hour or two on Sunday, but spend most of their week as if there is no death and no afterlife. They're only avoiding the inevitable.

Unless you're a genealogist, you're probably still scratching your head. When you're dead long enough, no matter how significant you thought you were, death has a way of turning our names into mud. That, too, is inevitable.

Because death is inevitable, there is no escaping it. Therefore, we need to have a solid grasp of what it means to die.

Stop for a minute and consider your views about death. Are you afraid to talk about it? What is it that scares you the most?

_____

_____

_____

_____

_____

_____

_____

Read Hebrews 9:27 again. What causes you the greater concern? Death, or the judgment that follows? Why?

_____

_____

_____

_____

_____

_____

_____

2. DEATH: WHAT IT MEANS

Because death is inevitable, there is no escaping it. Therefore, we need to have a solid grasp of what it means to die.

This is such an important event that you want to be sure you don't get the wrong idea from the wrong person's wrong opinion. So let's look at what the Bible has to say about two people who have died and stepped into the afterlife:

> "Now there was a rich man, and he habitually dressed in purple and fine linen, joyously living in splendor every day. And a poor man named Lazarus was laid at his gate, covered with sores, and longing to be fed with the crumbs, which were falling from the rich man's table; besides, even the dogs were coming and licking his sores. Now the poor man died and was carried away by the angels to Abraham's bosom; and the rich man also died and was buried. In Hades he lifted up his eyes, being in torment, and saw Abraham far away and Lazarus in his bosom. And he cried out and said, 'Father Abraham, have mercy on me and send Lazarus so that he may dip the tip of his finger in water and cool off my tongue, for I am in agony in this flame.'"
>
> Luke 16:19-24

It doesn't matter how much you make or who you are. The rich man died, and the poor man died. And both were equally dead.

Jesus' parable in Luke 16 involves two men a rich man and a poor man. The rich man was dressed in all the fancy clothes, and the poor man, Lazarus, was a beggar outside the gates.

Both men died, including the rich man. You can't drive enough cars, live in or buy enough homes, or take enough vacations to shake death from your trail. The rich man died. It doesn't matter how much you make or who you are. Check any cemetery; you can't tell one set of bones from another. The rich man died, and the poor man died-and both were equally dead.

Notice that the Bible uses a conjunction, not a period. Now, it would be easy to say, "The poor man died. The rich man died." But it says, "The poor man died ... *and* the rich man also died" (emphasis added). When both men died, it wasn't over. There was no period; there was a conjunction. One was carried to Abraham's bosom, and the other opened his eyes in torment in hell.

·Nowhere does the Bible say that those who die just don't exist anymore. In the Bible, the word death means "to separate."

So what does death really mean? The Bible's definition of death is not the same as the human definition. In the Bible, death means separation, not cessation. Nowhere does the Bible say that those who die just don't exist anymore. In the Bible, the word *death* means "to separate."

When you and I use the word *death*, we are talking about what James 2:26 calls the separation of our immaterial part from the material part ("The body without the spirit is dead.") A separation occurs. Why?

Think back to the Creation account in Genesis. God made Adam from the dust of the ground, and Adam was lifeless ... until God "breathed into his nostrils the breath of life; and man became a living being" (Genesis 2:7). God gave Adam a soul.

You are not who you are because of your body. You are who you are because of your soul. Two people may look alike-they may even be identical twins-but they are still two different people. They are not the same person because they have different souls. Your body is simply the material container for the immaterial part of who you are.

Every human being receives a soul at the point of conception. The soul is an immaterial part of us that is eternal in the sense that it will never cease to exist. When a person dies, the reason why it's not all over is that only the body dies; the soul doesn't die. Our souls are made to last forever. Therefore, they *cannot* die.

> If we want to know the truth about death and the afterlife, then we must put aside our feelings and look at God's Word.

Now, there are some people who believe that when we die, our souls just go to sleep. But that's not true. When we die, only our bodies go to sleep. Lazarus didn't go to sleep; he was carried away to Abraham's bosom. The rich man didn't go to sleep; he was carried away into eternal torment.

The Bible only gives us two options for the afterlife. People can come up with as many others as they want, but there are still only two real destinations to choose from.

This concept of the soul is hard to comprehend, but it's the truth. When your casket is carried into the church for your funeral, you aren't going to be there. Everyone else may show up, but you won't be able to make it. Sure, the people will come down that aisle and look into that old box as if you were somewhere in the vicinity, but let me tell you something: You'll be long gone.

> One thing heaven is not is a place of eternal boredom.

When a person dies, his or her soul is *immediately* separated from the body and delivered to one of two places. The Bible makes no mention whatsoever of a place called purgatory. It knows nothing of an intermediate zone where you can "get your stuff together." That in-between place has been passed down to some people through tradition, but the Bible says you either go up or down.

It's just like when two people get married. The word *married* doesn't mean the marriage is over, because the marriage has just begun. The afterlife is the same way. Once your time comes, there's no stopping to wait in a place called purgatory.

A famous tombstone reads this way: "Poor stranger, when you pass me by, as you are now, so once was I. As I am now, so you will be. So prepare for death and follow me." A person walked by and saw that tombstone. He scratched through the inscription and wrote instead, "To follow you I'm not content until I know which way you went." That person understood that death is a one-way trip!

> The Bible only gives us two options for the afterlife. People can come up with as many others as they want, but there are still only two real destinations to choose from.

People like to play games when it comes to death. They like to guess how it's going to be.

It is so amazing to me how everybody has an opinion on the subject. I was witnessing to a man one time, and he said to me, "Well, I believe that when you die, you're dead and that's it." I said, "Based on what?" He had a feeling, but it was not based on knowledge.

If we want to know the truth about death and the afterlife, then we must put aside our feelings and look at the revelation of God in His Word, because

He does speak on this subject. The Bible says both men were carried away, because death is separation, not cessation.

Read Luke 16:19-26. Based on what you read, is purgatory (an in-between place) an option when someone dies? Explain, using Scripture to support your answer.

_____

_____

_____

_____

_____

_____

_____

_____

_____

What was the basis of Paul's confidence when he talked about life after death? Read 2 Corinthians 5:6-8, then write your answer.

_____

_____

_____

_____

_____

_____

_____

_____

_____

3. DEATH: WHAT IT DOESN'T MEAN

When the word *bosom* is used, it makes us think, if you'll recall, the apostle John laid his on the bosom of the Lord at the Last Supper. So, because of Abraham's *bosom*, we can think of heaven as a place of eternal rest.

But one thing heaven is *not* is a place of eternal boredom. People will say, "What do you think you'll be doing in heaven all day? Flying around and playing the harp? How boring. Let me hang out with my friends in hell. Who wants to be bored all day long . . . forever?"

They almost have a point. If you have ever been bored for one week, you know it can be very traumatic. Think about being bored forever. Absolutely not! However, if you will catch a glimpse of the heaven described in the Bible, you'll see that there is not going to be one second of boredom there.

Nor is there a second of frustration, irritation, aggravation, illness, sickness, or depression. In fact, there will be eternal rest and eternal enjoyment. There will be so much enjoyment in heaven that God is going to get rid of the nighttime so you'll never miss seeing the enjoyment, and He's going to give us brand-new bodies so we will never get tired of all the joy.

The joy will be non-stop ... forever ...because that is how long it takes to uncover God. How fortunate and blessed we are, because He has

> Pick your best day, think back on the very best day of your life, and that will be hell compared to your first minute in heaven.

"made us alive together with Christ by grace you have been saved and raised us up with Him and seated us with Him in the heavenly places in Christ Jesus so that in the ages to come He might show

*the surpassing riches of His grace in kindness toward us in Christ
Jesus."*

Ephesians 2:5-7

> I won't have to get used to dying. By the
> time my doctor pronounces me dead, be-
> fore that flat line has made its way across
> that screen, I will have been ushered out of
> this body and ushered into the presence of
> the Lord.

So think back on the very best day of your life, and that will be hell compared
to your first minute in heaven.

Think with me for just a moment. How long did it take God to create the
heavens and the earth? Six days. Now, how long has it been since Jesus left
earth and went to heaven? About 2,000 years.

Now, if Jesus could create an earth in six days and come up with something like
where we live today, can you imagine what heaven must look like after He has
been there for 2,000 years? It will be staggering beyond our wildest dreams.

God allowed the apostle Paul to catch a glimpse of heaven while he was still on
earth. In one of his letters, Paul talked about the time he was stoned and left for
dead. God took him, snatched his soul to heaven, and let him return to earth to
talk about it. Pual said he "was caught up into Paradise and heard inexpressible
words, which a man is not permitted to speak" (2 Corinthians 1:4).

Have you ever seen something that you just didn't know how to explain? Paul
had no words to express what he had witnessed.

 the**Afterlife** 17

But just as it is written, "Things which eye has not seen and ear has not heard, and which have not entered the heart of man, all that God has prepared for those who love Him."

1 Corinthians 2:9

> Heaven only works if the Bible is telling the truth. Heaven only works if Jesus Christ wasn't lying. But Jesus Christ is not a liar. He is the eternal Son of God.

What I like about the afterlife is this: Before the doctor will have a chance to pronounce me dead, I'll already be in heaven. I won't have to get used to dying. By the time my doctor pronounces me dead, before that flat line has made its way across that screen, I will have been ushered out of this body and ushered into the presence of the Lord, where I will be awaiting my new body.

And that new body is going to be eternal, to keep up with my soul, which is already eternal, because I have trusted in the finished work of Jesus Christ.

Guess what? This preacher will never die. The good news about heaven is that I won't have to die to go there. In fact, when the Bible talks about Christians being dead, it uses the word *asleep*. Do you know why? Because the soul will already be in heaven, but the body is just waiting to be resurrected.

The believer in Jesus Christ does not need to fear death-because the believer in Jesus Christ will never experience it! The Bible says that the believer's "death" really means "to be absent from the body and to be at home with the Lord" (2 Corinthians 5:8).

The moment a Christian leaves his body, he doesn't go on a sightseeing tour of the universe, but he is immediately transported into the presence of God. Therefore, Christians will never experience the very thing that causes so many of us to fear.

Paul said, "But we do not want you to be uninformed, brethren, about those who are asleep, so that you will not grieve as do the rest who have no hope" (I Thessalonians 4:13). Yes, we cry for our loved ones who are not here, and that is very natural. But if your loved one belongs to Jesus, your cry should be a hopeful one, not a hopeless one.

Let me ask you a question. When you die, do you want a funeral service or a memorial service? I want a memorial service. I want everyone to party, party, party, because at that point that you are mourning over me, I will be more alive than I've ever been in my life. A memorial service just means "See you later." And if you know Jesus Christ as Lord, you will be more alive at that moment than when the doctor pronounced you dead.

> When we think of hell, we normally think about fiery flames and screaming. But in Hades, this man was having a conversation. So there's at least conscious awareness.

When Jesus was dying on the cross, there were two men beside him. One of those men recognized Jesus for who He was.

> *One of the criminals who were hanged there was hurling abuse at Him, saying, "Are You not the Christ? Save yourself and us! But the other answered, and rebuking him said, Do you not even fear God, since you are under the same sentence of condemnation? And we indeed are suffering justly, for we are receiving what we deserve for our deeds; but this man has done nothing wrong. And he was saying, Jesus, remember me when You come in Your kingdom! And He said to him, Truly I say to you, today you shall be with Me in Paradise.*
>
> *Luke 23:39-43*

Notice the word *today*. He didn't say *50 million years later.* He said *today*. As soon as you close your eyes, the angels will usher you into eternity. So if the doctor says the disease is terminal, you'll naturally cry tears.

But they won't be tears *without* hope; they'll be tears *with* hope. This is the way it was for Stephen in Acts 7. This man was experiencing rocks hitting him on the head, and he knew he was dying. But he had hope. And because of his hope, he caught a glimpse of heaven.

> *Now when they heard this they were cut to the quick, and they began gnashing their teeth at him. But being full of the Holy Spirit, he gazed intently into heaven and saw the glory of God, and Jesus standing at the right hand of God; and he said, 'Behold, I see the heavens opened up and the Son of Man standing at the right hand of God.'"*
>
> *Acts 7:54-56*

When it comes to death and the afterlife, you can't afford to be wrong.

Stephen caught a glimpse of heaven, and what did he see? Jesus Christ standing at the right hand of the Father! I wouldn't be surprised if Jesus was giving him a standing ovation. One of the great church fathers was dying, and the family was gathered around crying. Then he looked up and saw the heavens opened up.

Now, some people will say that they want to go to heaven, but that they don't need Jesus Christ to get there. But here's the hitch: Heaven only works if the Bible is telling the truth. Heaven only works if Jesus Christ wasn't lying. If heaven is not real, then Jesus Christ was a hypocrite and a liar.

And if that's the case, He is not worthy to be worshipped, not worthy to be adored. We could just close down the churches, sell the buildings, and do something else with our time. Because if heaven is not real, then we can't worship a liar. If heaven is not real, then we can't worship a hypocrite. If heaven is not real, then we can't worship a lunatic.

But Jesus Christ is not a liar. He's not a hypocrite. He's not a lunatic. He is the eternal Son of God, the King of kings, the Lord of lords. And we will worship Him.

Now, look back at Jesus' parable about the rich man and Lazarus. What do we see about the rich man's situation?

> Today, if you are a Christian, your present circumstances are the only hell you'll ever know. Today, if you are not a Christian, your present circumstances are the only heaven you'll ever know.

> *"And the rich man also died and was buried. In Hades he lifted up his eyes, being in torment, and saw Abraham far away and Lazarus in his bosom. And he cried out and said, 'Father Abraham, have mercy on me, and send Lazarus so that he may dip the tip of his finger in water and cool off my tongue, for I am in agony in this flame."*
>
> Luke 16:22

We can see what the afterlife is not, can't we? The man didn't stay dead, and he was not annihilated. But he was crying out for mercy.

When we think of hell, we normally think about fiery flames and people screaming. But here in Hades, this man was having an intelligent conversation. So there's at least conscious awareness. If you're there, you'll know it.

List some of the opinions you have heard about what happens to a person's soul when he or she dies.

_____

_____

_____

_____

_____

_____

_____

_____

_____

_____

_____

Read Luke 16:22-24; 23:43; 1 Corinthians2:9; and 2 Corinthians 5:8. What do these verses say about the afterlife?

_____

_____

_____

_____

_____

_____

_____

_____

_____

_____

4. DEATH: IT'S A DECISION

You may be shaking your head, saying, "Are you crazy? It's not going to be like that. You can't believe in a literal heaven and a literal hell. You're foolish to believe that."

> On the cross of Calvary, Jesus Christ took the sting out of death. And now all death can do to us is make a lot of noise. It cannot sting us, for it has lost its sting.

Maybe you think you know more than I do, and there is no hell. Maybe you think you know more than I do, and there is no life after death. All I can say to you is this: Don't be wrong. When it comes to death and the afterlife, you can't afford to be wrong.

Donald Grey Barnhouse was driving his kids home after his first wife's funeral, and one of the kids was confused. He was trying to make some sense of what had happened, and he said, "Daddy, I don't understand. Why did Mommy go? What's this thing called death?"

Barnhouse was trying to explain death and eternity, and suddenly a truck passed by and cast a shadow over their car. He looked back at his kids and said, "Kids, would you rather have been hit by the truck or the truck's shadow?" Well, of course, they said "the truck's shadow" because it doesn't hurt you; it just darkens you for a moment.

And then, in his wisdom, Barnhouse said, "Son, when you die without Christ, you get hit by the truck. When you die with Christ, you only get hit by the shadow."

This is precisely why we can say along with the psalmist, "Even though I walk through the valley of the shadow of death, I fear no evil, for You are with me; Your rod and Your staff, they comfort me" (Psalm 23:4).

When the rich man opened his eyes in Hades, he was in torment. Hell is punishment, and there are different degrees of punishment. It won't be the same for everybody.

Before making a decision about the afterlife, it is important for you to understand these things as well as the length of eternity. Let's say you drained the Pacific Ocean. There would be a big hole in the ground. Then let's say you filled the Pacific Ocean with sand.

> Eternity is waiting for anyone who will simply come to Jesus Christ for salvation. He died for us and then rose again on our behalf in order to give us salvation, at no cost to ourselves.

Now, Mount Everest is the highest mountain in the world. Let's say you made that sand pit of the Pacific Ocean as high as Mount Everest, the tallest mountain peak in the world. That would be one hefty pile of sand.

Now, let's say a bird flies over to that pile of sand and takes away one grain of it. How long would it take that bird to finish that sand pile? We don't have numbers that go that far. But when that bird takes its last grain of sand, we will only have been in eternity for one second. That's a long time to be wrong.

Today, if you are a Christian, your present circumstances are the only hell you'll ever know. Today, if you are *not* a Christian, your present circumstances are the only heaven you'll ever know. Don't play Russian roulette with eternity.

As long as the wheel is spinning, you can change your bet. But once the wheel stops, all bets are off. God has come up with a way to take the sting out of death. Though it still may be uncomfortable, He has removed its sting for His children.

> Have you considered the afterlife? The Bible is clear about our choices, and the decision is yours to make.

A father and son were in the car together one day when a bee flew into the vehicle. The boy panicked and began screaming, so the father reached out, grabbed the bee, and squeezed it in his hand. When he opened his hand, the bee flew away from him and continued buzzing around in the car.

The boy started screaming again, and the father said to him, "Son, you can stop screaming. You don't need to be afraid anymore." He then held out his hand to his son, and inside the palm of his hand was the bee's stinger.

On the cross of Calvary, Jesus Christ took that stinger so that we wouldn't have to. And now all death can do to us is make a lot of noise. It cannot sting us, for it has lost its sting.

Eternity is waiting for anyone who will simply come to Jesus Christ for salvation. He died for us and then rose again on our behalf in order to give us salvation. He paid the price so that we wouldn't have to.

So you have a decision to make. All you have to do is come by faith-not trusting in yourself, but trusting in Him. You can't trust your good life, your good works, or even your church membership. You must trust Him ... and only Him

What excuses have you (or someone you know) used for not making a decision to accept Jesus Christ as Savior and Lord?

_____

_____

_____

_____

_____

_____

_____

_____

_____

Look up Matthew 3:2; 4:17; 7:13-14; Mark 1:15; John 1:12; 3:16, 18; 6:40, 47; 11:25-26; and Romans 10:9-10. What does the Bible say about man's responsibility for his eternal destiny?

_____

_____

_____

_____

_____

_____

_____

_____

_____

_____

The afterlife offers us one of two choices, and I have chosen heaven. But I won't go there because I have been a good person or because I have served as pastor or a teacher. I'm only going there because I have placed my trust and my eternal destiny in the nail-pierced hands of Jesus Christ.

What about you? Have you thought about death? Have you considered the afterlife? The Bible is clear about our choices, and the decision is yours to make.

> *"I am the resurrection and the life; he who believes in Me will live even if he dies, and everyone who lives and believes in Me will never die. Do you believe this?"*
>
> John 11:25-26

Consider the words of the One who removed the sting of death for you. Do you believe this? The afterlife is real. The decision is yours. You can't afford to be wrong on this one.

NOTES

— NOTES —

L E S S O N   2
WHAT IS HEAVEN?

In My Father's house...

are many dwelling places; if it were not so, I would have told you; for I go to prepare a place for you. - John 14:1-3

Many people are confused when it comes to heaven. Most people even, some Christians, view the thought of heaven as an intrusion into their lives. After all, why focus on heaven if you haven't even been to Europe? Many single people try to skirt the issue, saying, "Lord, please, don't take me to heaven until I get married down here on earth."

Why the hesitation? Why the reluctance? It's because people are confused. There are some of us who seem to think that heaven is a big pie-in-the-sky existence, where you just flap your wings and float from cloud to cloud.

Some even say, "It's going to be so boring. How can it be exciting when you know you are going to make a hole-in-one every time? We'll never miss a basket, never have a conflict. It's going to be so boring." That's one extreme. The other extreme is so secularized that it is totally unlike anything God ever had in mind.

The Scriptures do not tell us everything about heaven. In fact, all we have in the Scriptures are glimpses of heaven. But those glimpses are enough to let us know that heaven is where we want to go.

I'm just as anxious as you are to get into what we're going to do there, what it's going to look like, and all the rest, but we need to pause before we do that and just ask this simple question: What is heaven?

1. HEAVEN IS A PROMISED PLACE

In John 14, Jesus had been preparing His disciples for His death, burial, resurrection, and ascension to the Father. They were devastated about His going away, and they wanted to know how they were going to make it in His absence.

Jesus wanted to comfort them, just as He wants to comfort you. So He gave His disciples and us a glimpse of heaven:

> *"Do not let your heart be troubled; believe in God; believe also in Me. In My Father's house are many dwelling places; if it were not so, I would have told you; for I go to prepare a place for you. If I go and prepare a place for you I will come again and receive you to Myself; that where I am there you may be also."*
>
> *John 14:1-3*

He said He was going to prepare a place for them, and that place is called heaven. Therefore, heaven is a promised place because it is based on a promise.

Now, a promise is only as good as the one who makes the promise. It depends on the person making the promise and his or her integrity to make good on the promise.

Jesus wanted to comfort His disciples, just as He wants to comfort you. So He gave them and us- a glimpse of heaven.

First of all, Jesus said that the promise depends on the character of God. He said to "believe in God." If you have doubts about the reality of heaven, just believe

God. If you doubt that heaven is really a place, just believe God. The reality of the promise of heaven is tied to the person of God. To put it another way, if heaven is a lie, then God is a liar. And if God is a liar, then we can stop believing anything and everything else that God has ever said. Jesus wants us to "believe in God." The character of God is trustworthy. We can bet our lives on His character. In Paul's letter to Titus, he refers to his "God, who cannot lie" (Titus 1:2). We can trust the character of God.

We learn in 2 Corinthians 5:1 that "if the earthly tent which is our house is torn down, we have a building from God, a house not made with hands, eternal in the heavens." God has prepared us a home in heaven.

The same God who created the heavens and the earth in Genesis 1 is the same God who promises us a new heaven and a new earth at the end of time (Revelation 21:1).

Not only is heaven a promised place that is tied to the character of God, but it is also tied to the character of His Son, Jesus Christ. He said, "Believe in God, believe also in Me."

> The closer you get to Christ, the closer you get to heaven; the closer you get to Christ, the more you will see Him working in your life.

This statement must have been very meaningful to the disciples. They had walked with Him for three years and had seen Him perform mighty miracles. They had watched Him give sight to the blind, make the lame to walk, cause the dumb to talk, and even walk on water.

In other words, we can't see God, but they *did* see Christ. So even if God is not concrete enough for you, Jesus says, "Believe also in Me." We are to believe in the Son of Man, who is Himself God in the flesh (see John I:18).

Jesus Christ is God wearing skin. The closer you get to Christ, the closer you get to heaven; the closer you get to Christ, the more you will see Him working in your life. The more you see Christ working in your life, the more real He will become. And the more real He becomes, you won't doubt heaven because you won't doubt Him. Intimacy with Jesus Christ brings reality to the invisible God, giving us a second confirmation of the reality of heaven.

> The promise of heaven, however, rests not only on the character of God the Father and Jesus Christ the Son, but also on the integrity of Scripture. The Bible is filled with glimpses of heaven.

The other thing Christ gives us is Somebody who can feel what we feel and understand what we understand, because He has gone through what we have gone through, and He can relate to us.

God the Father cannot relate to death, but Jesus the Son can-because He died. So He understands the transition process. He has been there, so we can call on Him.

The promise of heaven, however, rests not only on the character of God the Father and Jesus Christ the Son, but also on the integrity of Scripture. The Bible is filled with glimpses of heaven.

First, our citizenship is in heaven. "For our citizenship is in heaven, from which also we eagerly wait for a Savior, the Lord Jesus Christ" (Philippians 3:20).

Second, our inheritance and reservations are in heaven. God has caused us "to obtain an inheritance which is imperishable and undefiled and will not fade away, reserved in heaven for you" (1 Peter 4).

When I call a hotel and make reservations, I don't have to see the hotel to know that the reservations are firm. In fact, the way I know my reservations are firm is the confirmation number they give me. Then I take it by faith that the hotel will provide me with a room in that city at that time. Or if they don't, and I have a confirmation number, they'll find something to take care of me somehow.

This is good news, isn't it? Because we have already made our reservations in heaven, there is a room waiting for us. And we already have the confirmation number. It was written in the blood of Jesus Christ.

> The Old Testament saints mentioned in Hebrews were living on the earth, but they had their sights set on heaven. And when you become passionate about heaven, you will be fulfilled in history. The reason why many of us are unhappy on this earth is that we do not have a view of heaven.

Third, our reward is in heaven.
"Rejoice and be glad, for your reward in heaven is great" (Matthew 5:12a). No matter how successful we are in this life, we are only paupers compared to the reservations that have been made in heaven.

Fourth, our names are recorded in heaven. "Nevertheless do not rejoice in this, that the spirits are subject to you, but rejoice that your names are recorded in heaven" (Luke 10:20).

And, of course, we must not overlook the Old Testament saints, who were so passionate about God's dwelling place:

> All these died in faith, without receiving the promises, but having seen them and having welcomed them from a distance, and having

confessed that they were strangers and exiles on the earth. For those who say such things make it clear that they are seeking a country of their own. And indeed if they had been thinking of that country from which they went out, they would have had opportunity to return. But as it is, they desire a better country, that is, a heavenly one. Therefore God is not ashamed to be called their God; for He has prepared a city for them. Hebrews 11:13-16

The Old Testament saints mentioned in Hebrews were living on the earth, but they had their sights set on heaven. And when you become passionate about heaven, you will be fulfilled in history. The reason why many of us are unhappy on this earth is that we do not have a view of heaven.

> Heaven is pulsating with life, so to be passionate about heaven is to be fulfilled while waiting to go.

Now, a view of heaven does not mean that we become morbid, wanting to die, thinking about death all the time. It's just the opposite. It means we're thinking about life all the time. Heaven is pulsating with life, so to be passionate about heaven is to be fulfilled while waiting to go there. To be passionate about this earth is to be unfulfilled while waiting to go to heaven. So if we want to enjoy heaven or if we want to enjoy earth, we need to think about heaven. We need to learn about it from the great saints of old who were passionate about heaven even as they lived on this earth.

Heaven is a reality because it is based on the integrity of God the Father, God the Son, and the Scriptures, which were authored and inspired by God the Holy Spirit.

Read the following Scriptures, then record what you learn in the notes section of this study guide. Note which promises God has made and whether He has kept them or broken them.

PROMISE	WHAT HAPPENED
Genesis 18:9-14	Genesis 21:1-2
1 Kings 3:9-12	1 Kings 5:12
1 Chronicles 28:5-6	1 Kings 8:20
	2 Kings 8:19
Genesis 15:18-21	Nehemiah 9:8
Jeremiah 22:8-9	Jeremiah 40:1-3
Acts 1:4-5	Acts 2:33

What promises of God are still waiting to be fulfilled? Read James 1:12; 2:5; 1 John 2:25; and 2 Peter 3:13. Record your answers, then add them to the list you made in the notes section.

_____

_____

_____

_____

_____

_____

_____

_____

Will these promises be fulfilled? What does God's Word say about the promises He makes? Read 1 Kings 8:56; Romans 4:21; and 2 Peter 3:9. Record your answers, then add them to the separate list you are making.

_____

_____

_____

_____

_____

_____

_____

_____

_____

_____

2. HEAVEN IS A PARTICULAR PLACE

Heaven is not just a concept. It's not where we float around in Never-Never Land.
It's a particular place. Jesus said, "I go to prepare a place" for us (John 14:2).

> Heaven is a reality because it is based on the integrity of God the Father, God the Son, and the Scriptures, which were authored and inspired by God the Holy Spirit.

The Bible says that there are actually three heavens. In 2 Corinthians 12:2, Paul said he "was caught up to the third heaven."

Oftentimes, the Bible uses the plural word *heavens*. The first heaven is the atmospheric heaven or the realm in which man lives, the realm in which we breathe oxygen, the realm of the clouds. The second heaven is the stellar or planetary heaven. We would call it outer space, where the planets are, where the galaxy is huge. I believe that's where the angels operate.

And then there is the third heaven, which is what we're usually referring to when we talk about heaven. This heaven is the place where God dwells. When Jesus ascended after His resurrection, He had to go through the first two heavens to get to the third heaven, and that is where He is today, at the right hand of the Father.

When Jesus Christ ascended into heaven, He went *somewhere*. If I say I'm going to Los Angeles, I'm going somewhere. If I say I'm going to San Francisco, I'm going somewhere. When Jesus said "I go to prepare a place for you," He meant He was going somewhere.

How does the Lord's Prayer begin? "Our Father who is in heaven" (Matthew 6:9). Jesus constantly reminded His listeners that His Father is in heaven (see Matthew 10:32-33). Isaiah says God dwells "on a high and holy place" (Isaiah 57:15).

> The third heaven is the place where God dwells. When Jesus ascended after His resurrection, He had to go through the first two heavens to get to the third heaven, and that is where He is today, at the right hand of the Father.

Also, look at what the Bible shows us in 1 Kings 8:27: "But will God indeed dwell on the earth? Behold, heaven and the highest heaven cannot contain You, how much less this house which I have built!"

Solomon was dedicating the temple, and he basically said, "This temple cannot hold you, God. You are too big for this house. You know, God, even the heavens cannot contain You." This is interesting. God is bigger than heaven; He must be bigger than heaven because He is the one who created it. So when we talk with God, we are talking with Someone who is bigger than the universe He created.

If we try to explain the fact that God is bigger than the sum total of His galaxies, that God cannot be contained in His universe, we'll go crazy. We

All of heaven is not described for us in the Bible because it's just too big, so God has given us a glimpse of heaven by showcasing one city.

just have to believe it. God is bigger than the sum total of His creation.

How can we relate to a God like that? Well, God has already taken care of that. Because our understanding and comprehension is limited, God has given us just a snippet of heaven in the Bible.

This is why the Bible talks about "a city." Whenever you see the word city used, just think of it as the capital of heaven. Think of it as downtown heaven. All of heaven is not described for us in the Bible because it's just too big, so God has given us a glimpse of heaven by showcasing one city.

While most of us can't even relate to our whole country, we can relate to a city. And what a city it is!

> And he carried me away in the Spirit to a great and high mountain
> and showed me the holy city Jerusalem coming down out of heav-
> en from God having the glory of God. Her brilliance was like a very
> costly stone as a stone of crystal-clear jasper...And the city has no
> need of the sun or of the moon to shine on it, for the glory of God
> has illumined it, and its lamp is the Lamb.
>
> *Revelation 21:10-11, 23*

We have never seen anything like this place called heaven. Ezekiel caught a glimpse of it, but he couldn't come up with words to describe it. All he could say is that he saw lights flashing and wheels turning. It was beyond his ability even to come up with the right language to describe this place. When Paul caught a glimpse of heaven, he said he saw things "which a man is not per-mitted to speak" (2 Corinthians 12:4).

Heaven is not an idea; heaven is a place. It is a promised place that is tied to the character of the Father, the Son, and the Spirit, and it is a particular place-because God dwells there.

Why is it so significant that heaven is a place instead of a concept?

_____

_____

_____

_____

_____

_____

_____

_____

_____

_____

_____

What other theories about the afterlife have you heard or read about? How do those theories compare with what the Bible says?

_____

_____

_____

_____

_____

_____

_____

_____

_____

3. HEAVEN IS A PATERNAL PLACE

Heaven is more than a promise or a particular destination, though. It is also a paternal place. "In my Father's house are many dwelling places" (John 14:2).

Heaven is not an idea; heaven is a place. It is a promised place that is tied to the character of the Father, the Son, and the Spirit, and it is a particular place—because God dwells there.

In other words, heaven is a family affair. It's a family gathering of a Daddy and His kids. The term *dwelling places* is better-translated *apartments*. So there are many places to live for the many people who are going there.

Have you considered the details of the capital city? It is 1,500 miles around and 1,500 miles high-and this is just the capital! The city doesn't just go out, but it goes up; levels of streets go out and up; and the city is big enough to house billions of people.

The size of this one city is about the size of almost half of the United States, and that's just at ground level. There are layers in heaven with see-through streets-no concrete or tar will be needed. What God wants us to see is that this one city is just a staggering sight. And Jesus calls it the Father's house.

There are two important factors in the Father's house: First, only the Father's children get to live there. Second, the house reflects the character of the Daddy who lives there.

I have a great father, and I love him to death. My father has taken the old inner-city house that I grew up in, and that he's still living in today, and made it the best possible place it could be, given the community it is located in. Since he never wanted to move, he is in that same house, and so that's my father's house.

When we go home, I go home to my daddy's house. And when I go home to my daddy's house, it reflects the character of my dad because he wants his kids around him in his house.

Now, my father has limited power. He can't do everything he wants to do. So there are limits to what he can and cannot do in his house. However, God is not limited, and He can do anything He wants to do whenever He wants to do it. Can you imagine our heavenly Father's house?

If we have limited information about God, then we will have a limited appreciation for heaven right now, because we have to know our heavenly Father in order to understand what it's like to be at home with Him.

Maybe you didn't grow up with a father and therefore can't appreciate him in what he has done. Let me assure you, you have a Father in heaven who is always at home. In fact, His home is consumed with Him.

> There are two important factors in the Father's house: First, only the Father's children get to live there. Second, the house reflects the character of the Daddy who lives there.

Revelation 21:22 says, "I saw no temple in it, for the Lord God the Almighty and the Lamb are its temple." There will be no churches in heaven, because heaven is just one big church.

> If we have limited information about God, then we will have a limited appreciation for heaven right now, because we have to know our heavenly Father in order to understand what it's like to be at home with Him.

When Isaiah caught a glimpse of heaven, he saw the consuming presence of God. Heaven is where the glory of God shines unabated. It is where God fully expresses Himself, unhindered by sin. Every day we see a beautiful day, we say, "This is sure a gorgeous day!" Well, guess what? The most gorgeous of days we see on this earth are limited in beauty for two reasons. First, the earth's beauty is hampered by sin. Second, God works through other agencies. He works through the sun to give us sunshine, and He works through the moon to give us light at night. This is not so in heaven.

In heaven, there won't be any sin to hamper the beautiful days God has created. Our brightest days down here are gloomy and dark when compared to what's awaiting us in heaven. And not only will God *not* work through intermediary agencies such as the sun and moon, but He Himself will be the light.

God is the Creator, so He is brighter than the sun. And He will fully express Himself without working through an intermediary so that we can see the undiminished glory of God. It will be staggering.

If you are a believer in Jesus Christ, how does God see you?
Read Romans 8:16-17 and Ephesians 1:5, then record your answer.

_____

_____

_____

_____

_____

_____

If you are a believer in Jesus Christ, how does God want you to see Him? Read Matthew 6:9 and Romans 8:15, then record your answer. (Abba is equivalent to the English word Daddy, or Father.)

_____

_____

_____

_____

_____

_____

4. HEAVEN IS A POPULATED PLACE

What about the inhabitants of heaven? The Author of Hebrews offers some insight into who resides there:

> But you have come to Mount Zion and to the city of the living God, the heavenly Jerusalem, and to myriads of angels, to the general assembly and church of the first born who are enrolled in heaven, and to God, the Judge of all, and to the spirits of the righteous made

In heaven, there won't be any sin to hamper the beautiful days God has created. Our brightest days down here are gloomy and dark when compared to what's awaiting us in heaven.

perfect, and to Jesus, the mediator of a new covenant, and to the sprinkled blood, which speaks better than the blood of Abel.

Hebrews 12:22-24

Myriads of angels make up the first group living in heaven. We cannot see those angels now, but we will be able to see them in heaven because we will then have a spiritual body. The second group in heaven is the general assembly and church of the firstborn. This is the Christian church. So your spiritual family is there.

A church member came up to me one time and asked me, "Will you know me in heaven?" The truth is, I really won't know you *until* we get to heaven. I cannot fully know you now; I can only know what I see and what you tell me. Those are the only two things that I can know about you.

And what I see is not all that there is. I see you coming, so I ask you, "How are you doing?" You say, "Fine." And you're lying through your teeth. But unless I see differently, I can only deal with what I see and hear. Once we get to heaven, there will be a total removal of all facades, a total removal of all shams, and I will get to see you as God created you to be.

You can go down to the corner of Gold Street and Silver Boulevard and run into Abraham. You can say, "Hey, Abe, can I ask you a few questions?" Or, "So, Jonah, how did it feel living inside a fish for three days?"

One of the amazing things about the population in heaven is that everybody will fulfill his potential. Isn't that something? All of us are going to die with things unfulfilled-things that we hope to do in our businesses that we never got done, things that we hope to do with our kids that we never got done, things we hoped to do, things we dreamed about doing.

Heaven won't be a boring place, yet there won't be any crabs in the barrel, there won't be anyone trying to pull us down, and there won't be a rival group in heaven.

> Heaven is being built with you and me in mind. Trust me, you're going to love the decorating.

In fact, you'll want to meet some of the people there. You can go down to the corner of Gold Street and Silver Boulevard and run into Abraham. You can say, "I Iey, Abe, can I ask you a few questions?" Or, "David, tell me how you threw that stone up the side of Goliath's big head." Or, "So, Jonah, how did it feel living inside a fish for three days?" You'll be able to get into everybody's business. Because the church will have fellowship with the souls of the spirits of men made perfect, or Old Testament saints, we will be able to hang out and have dinner with Adam or go shopping with Eve. We will be able to get to know people we have only heard and read about.

In that passage from Hebrews, we learn that Someone else will be in heaven as well: "and to Jesus, the mediator of a new covenant, and to the sprinkled blood, which speaks better than the blood of Abel" (Hebrews 12:24).

Our Savior is there. God is there. The angels are there. The church of Jesus Christ is there. The Old Testament saints are there. It's a busy place. Billions of people will be there, because these are all the believers who have ever lived. Yet there will be no crowding and no sin. This is what heaven is.

Who will we see when we get to heaven (Hebrews 12:22-23)?

_____

_____

_____

_____

_____

_____

_____

_____

Who are the first people you want to see when you get there?

_____

_____

_____

_____

_____

_____

_____

_____

5. HEAVEN IS A PREPARED PLACE

When Jesus ascended to the Father, He went to prepare a place for us. It's amazing—He's preparing a place just for us.

And not only is He preparing a place for _us_, but He is specifically preparing a place for _you_. He is specifically preparing a place for _me_.

Heaven is being built with you and me in mind. Trust me, you're going to love the decorating. It's all-indicative of your individual personality, interests, and tastes.

Heaven and earth are about to undergo some remodeling, some major renovations.

> "But the day of the Lord will come like a thief, in which the heavens will pass away with a roar and the elements will be destroyed with intense heat and the earth and its works will be burned up."
>
> 2 Peter 3:10

So God is going to renovate this heaven and this earth with intense heat. This heaven and this earth will be gutted, and the rest of

> If you want the best that the after-life has to offer, if you have caught a glimpse of heaven and you want to go there, Jesus Christ would love to take you there.

heaven and earth will look like the new Jerusalem of Revelation 21. That's why we can't get bored for a billion years. The new heaven and new earth will all merge together in one glorious revelation of God. It will be spectacular.

Read 1 Corinthians 2:9. Write out a prayer to God, thanking Him for the preparations He has made for us.

_____

_____

_____

_____

_____

_____

_____

_____

_____

_____

_____

What other preparations has God made for His people? Look up the following verses, then record your answer: Matthew 25:34; Luke 2:30-31; Ephesians 2:10; and Hebrews 11:16.

_____

_____

_____

_____

_____

_____

_____

_____

_____

_____

_____

_____

6. HEAVEN IS A PERSONAL PLACE

Not only is heaven a promised place, a particular place, a paternal place, a populated place, and a prepared place, but heaven is a personal place. Jesus said in John 14:3, "I'll go and prepare a place for you, I will come again and receive you to Myself, that where I am, there you may be also."

Jesus is coming again...unless He's a liar. But do you know what? If Jesus Christ rose from the dead-and He did-then there won't be any problem when He gets ready to return.

He has ascended to the Father and is preparing a place for us. When the fullness of time comes, He will come again and receive us to Himself. Now, that's personal.

Before we get too high on heaven, Jesus Christ wants us to get high on something else-being with Him. You see, being with Him is the heart of heaven. It's what it's all about.

Heaven is being with the Savior. That's what will make heaven *heavenly*. Yes, it will be nice to go to a spectacular environment; yes, it will be nice not to have any nighttime; yes, it will be nice not to have any more thunderstorms; yes, it will be nice to eat and never get full or overweight; yes, it will be nice to talk to folks and not misunderstand them and get upset with them; yes, it will be nice to live in the apartment God has waiting for us. But the reason we are going to heaven is simply because Jesus wants us to *be with Him*.

The closer you are to Christ now, the more precious heaven will look then. That relationship will make heaven *heaven* The place itself will just be the backdrop for that relationship. It'll just be the scenery behind the central picture of you and your Savior, of me and my Savior, hand in hand for all eternity.

Thomas was excited about all this, and he wanted to know more. As you read Thomas's question and Jesus' answer, just take a minute to savor what is being said.

> *"If I go and prepare a place for you, I will come again and receive you to Myself, that where I am, there you may be also. And you know the way where I am going" Thomas said to Him, 'Lord, we do not know where You are going, how do we know the way?" Jesus said to him, I am the way, and the truth, and the life; no one comes to the Father but through Me'."*
>
> *John 14:3-6*

Thomas wanted to go, but he didn't know how. He didn't know the way. Jesus said, "I am the way." No one will ever see the Father except through the Son.

LESSON 2

What makes heaven *heaven?*

_____

_____

_____

_____

_____

_____

_____

_____

_____

_____

_____

_____

_____

Based on your answer above, what make *hell* hell?

_____

_____

_____

_____

_____

_____

_____

_____

_____

_____

_____

You want to go to heaven? Do you know that you're going to heaven? Jesus is the only One who knows where heaven is. He is the only One who knows exactly how to get there. He is the only One who knows the Father's standards. He is the only One who can get you in. So we have to go through Him.

If you want the best that the afterlife has to offer, if you have caught a glimpse of heaven and you want to go there, Jesus Christ would love to take you there. And we can safely entrust our eternal destiny to Him.

NOTES

LESSON 3
WHAT IS HEAVEN LIKE?

Then he showed me...

a river of the water of life, clear as crystal, coming from the throne of God and of the Lamb, in the middle of its street.

A boy from the ghetto was standing outside talking to a very elegant woman who lived in one of the downtown skyscrapers.

The two just stood staring at the beautiful building, and then the boy turned his attention to the woman.

In heaven, everything is brand-new all the time. Nothing ever gets old, and there are never any negative interruptions. Heaven is always new.

"Miss, may I ask you a question?" he asked.

"Yes," she replied.

"Which one of those buildings is your project?" he asked.

"Project?!" she exclaimed.

"That's a *high rise!* How dare you call that a *project?!"*

Brothers and sisters in Christ, in light of what God has in store for you, anywhere you live on this earth is just a project. The magnificence awaiting us in heaven is beyond words.

> God is going to remove every fiber that has been affected by sin and fundamentally renovated it. He will renovate the universe of sin and all of its effects and remake everything.

Paul was allowed a glimpse of heaven, but he had no words to express what he saw. He "was caught up into Paradise and heard inexpressible words, which a man is not permitted to speak" (2 Corinthians 12:4).

There is no language to clarify, explain, or articulate what heaven is like. All the sermons of all the preachers of all time are like dust, because heaven is inexpressible.

Yet God has given us His Word, and in His Word are just a few tidbits, just a small sample, just a little taste of the glory of heaven.

1. HEAVEN IS PERFECT

Fundamentally, at the core of heaven, is the removal of the curse. At the core of heaven is the reversal of sin's effect on this world. Revelation 21 and 22 show us the reversal of what happened in Genesis 3.

The events of Genesis 3 produced a curse that has affected this entire world that God created. Because of this curse, God's world can never be fully enjoyed. God had heaven in mind when He created the world. He created the earth *heavenly.*

Sin interrupted that, and that is why every time you begin to enjoy something, something goes wrong. The new car gets old. The new marriage gets old. The new baby gets old. The new job gets old. The new house gets old. Why? Because everything that happens is under the curse. Everything that happens is affected by the presence of sin in the world. People look for new thrills because the old thrills have gotten old. The new thrills do not last under the curse.

But in heaven, there will be no more curse because there will be no more sin nor its effect. And because there is no more curse, because there is no more sin, "He who sits on the throne said, 'Behold, I am making all things new'" (Revelation 21:5).

In heaven, everything is brand-new all the time. Nothing ever gets old, and there are never any negative interruptions. So whatever heaven is, it is always new.

> Out of all its perfections, I believe the first thing we'll notice when we get to heaven is its beauty.

How will God make everything new? "But the day of the Lord will come like a thief, in which the heavens will pass away with a roar and the elements will be destroyed with intense heat, and the earth and its works will be burned up....(2 Peter 3:10, 12). But, according to His promise, we are looking for a new heaven and a new earth in which righteousness dwells.

From a physics standpoint, God could do this by simply splitting every atom in the universe. Whenever every atom is split, what we'll have is a universal Nagasaki or a universal Hiroshima.

However He chooses to do it, God is going to remove every fiber that has been affected by sin and fundamentally renovate it. He will renovate the universe of sin and all of its effects and remake everything.

When this time comes, the curse will be lifted and heaven will be realized as the eternal experience of God's perfection. God is perfect, so what He will let us do is spend all eternity enjoying what His perfection is like. We'll come to enjoy His perfection in a place called heaven and in an experience we have come to know as paradise.

God has promised that in heaven, all things will become new. Have you experienced His ability to turn old into new? If so, how? Read 2 Corinthians 5:17, then record your answer.

_____

_____

_____

_____

_____

_____

_____

_____

_____

_____

Do you feel the effect sin has had on the world around you? What will it mean to you for God to make all things new?

_____

_____

_____

_____

_____

_____

_____

_____

_____

_____

_____

_____

2. HEAVEN IS PERFECT BEAUTY

Out of all its perfections, I believe the first thing we will notice when we get to heaven is its beauty.

> 'When I saw a new heaven and a new earth; for the first heaven and the first earth passed away and there is no longer any sea. And I saw the holy city new Jerusalem coming down out of heaven from God made ready as a bride adorned for her husband.
>
> *Revelation 21:1-2*

When New Jerusalem— this capital of the new heaven and new earth—is revealed, get ready, because we are all going to say, "Ohhhh!"

God uses the very best picture to describe to us what the dawning of this new day will be like. It's going to be like a wedding day.

When the bride comes down the center aisle on her wedding day, the audience stands in awe. As she makes her way down that aisle, we see that she is flawless. She has gone through great preparation in the bridal room to make sure that every detail is covered-no wrinkles, no spots, and perfect makeup. As she moves down the aisle, we watch with anticipation.

Rarely do I attend a wedding where someone in the audience doesn't see the bride and say, "Ohhhhh!" As she shows up at the door, we are waiting to exhale. We are just overwhelmed and overcome with the staggering beauty entering the room.

When New Jerusalem—this capital of the new heaven and new earth—is revealed, get ready, because we are all going to say, "Ohhhhh!" We will not have words to express this adorning that will take place. God doesn't describe all of heaven in His Word, but He describes for us this capital city in Revelation 21:10-27.

First, it will be spacious. Verse 16 says, "The city is laid out as a square, and its length is as great as the width; and he measured the city with the rod, fifteen hundred miles; its length and width and height are equal."

Fifteen hundred miles is from the Atlantic Ocean to the Rockies. That is half of the United States of America. It's from Canada to Mexico. So create a box from the Atlantic to the Rockies and from Canada to Mexico, and you've got the idea of the size of the city.

Do you remember how Jesus said He was going away to prepare a place for us? This is the place! This is where you and I, because we are believers in Jesus Christ, are going to live forever and ever!

And the city is just as tall as it is wide. So we have this city that is half the size of America in length and half the size of America in height. This is a high-rise like we've never seen before.

A great and high wall surrounds this magnificent city, and this wall has 12 gates bearing the names of the 12 tribes of Israel because the Old Testament saints live in this city (v. 12).

Not only that, but verse 19 says that the foundation stones of the city wall will be adorned with every kind of precious stone. Notice the description of this place:

The material of the wall was jasper; and the city was pure gold like clear glass. The foundation stones of the city wall were adorned with every kind of precious stone. The first foundation stone was jasper; the second, sapphire; the third, chalcedony; the fourth, emerald; the fifth, sardonyx; the sixth, sardius; the seventh, chrysolite; the eighth, beryl; the ninth, topaz; the tenth, chrysoprase; the eleventh, jacinth; the twelfth, amethyst. And the twelve gates were twelve pearls; each one of the gates was a single pearl. And the street of the city was pure gold like transparent glass.

Revelation 21:10-21

There will never be any time when the beauty of heaven will not be able to be seen and enjoyed—because it is always daytime!

Why 12 pearly gates? Jesus had 12 tribes in the Old Testament, and He had 12 apostles in the New Testament. *Twelve* is a number that represents the Old Testament saints and the New Testament church.

Do you remember how Jesus said He was going away to prepare a place for us? This is the place! This is where you and I, because we are believers in Jesus Christ, are going to live forever and ever! And it will be nothing short of spectacular.

This one city can house billions of people. The walls are 216 feet high, and the gates are just as huge. This city will be one gigantic jewel. The whole city is a jewel. But this jewel is unlike anything we have ever worn on our bodies. This jewel has "the glory of God. Her brilliance was like a very costly stone, as a stone of crystal-clear jasper" (v. ll).

We will be able to behold beauty that is unimaginable. And not only will we be able to behold it, but we will not be able to *not* behold it.

And the city has no need of the sun or of the moon to shine on it for the glory of God has illumined it and its lamp is the Lamb. ...And there will no longer be any night; and they will not have need of the light of a lamp nor the light of the sun because the Lord God will illumine them and they will reign forever and ever.

Revelation 21:23; 22:5

Not only is heaven a place of perfect beauty, but it is a place of perfect worship.

There will never be any time when the beauty of heaven will not be able to be seen and enjoyed-because it is always daytime!

There is no nighttime, there is no sleeping, and there is no need of electricity, because God's glory will be unencumbered. The sun and moon may be there, but they won't be necessary. All they will do is reflect the glory of the stones.

God is creating this city so that it can absorb His glory and beam it back off. This glory will be reflected. So when we see the glory of God in the street, we will see the glory of God bounce off the street. When we see the glory of God hit the walls, we will see the glory of God bounce off the walls. Not only will we see the glory, but we will walk in the glory. It will be totally consumed with one gigantic jewel.

Read Genesis 1:1-5, then list everything you learn about the light. Now read Genesis 1:14-19. What was the light in verse 3?

_____

_____

_____

_____

_____

Read Revelation 21:10-21, then roughly sketch what you have read about. When you finish, thank God for the eternal home He has prepared for you.

_____

_____

_____

_____

_____

_____

_____

3. HEAVEN IS PERFECT WORSHIP

Not only is heaven a place of perfect beauty, but it is also a place of perfect worship.

> And I heard a loud voice from the throne, saying, "Behold, the tabernacle of God is among men, and He will dwell among them, and they shall be His people, and God Himself will be among them."
>
> Revelation 21:3

It won't be that we're in church all day long, forever. But what we'll be doing throughout eternity is reflecting who and what God is. That is true worship.

The tabernacle is where the Old Testament saints worshiped God. The saints went to the tabernacle for worship because it was a place that reminded them of God.

Why do we need to go to church? For the same reason—to be reminded of God. Our enemy, Satan, tries to get us to forget everything as soon as we step outside the church doors, and he fights with us all week long.

There will be no churches in this new city because the city *is* the church. The New Jerusalem is the tabernacle that comes down out of heaven.

Now, some of you may be reading this and thinking, "Are you kidding me? Won't I ever get to take a break from church?" If this is what you're saying, I understand. But you're saying this because you don't understand worship.

> There will never be a time when He's distant or far off. There will never be a time when we feel alone or disconnected. We will be high on God—all the time.

Worship was never meant to be going to a building once a week. Worship was meant to be this: "Whether, then, you eat or drink or whatever you do, do all to the glory of God" (1 Corinthians 10:31).

It won't be that we're in church all day long, forever. But what we'll be doing throughout eternity is reflecting who and what God is. That is true worship.

We worship when we drink water and give Him glory. We worship when we eat food and give Him glory. We worship when we get dressed and say, "Lord, thank You that I am not naked today." We give Him glory and worship when we thank Him that we didn't have to walk because He gave us a car.

Worship is giving God glory, and since the city will be the sanctuary, every place we go, everything we do, and every time we have a conversation about worship, will be worship. It will encompass all of life, for the city is the tabernacle. Worship will be what it was meant to be.

Oh, how wonderful it's going to be! Can you just imagine? There will never be a time when God's presence won't impact you, because you will be walking in

His reflected glory all the time. There will never be a time when He's distant or far off. There will never be a time when we feel alone or disconnected. We will be high on God all the time.

The Greek word for "worship" is *proskuneo*, which literally means, "to throw a kiss." Does this definition apply to your personal worship? If so, how?

The Word of God makes a distinction between two kinds of worship, saying that one is better than the other. Which is better? Read I Samuel 15:22, then record your answer.

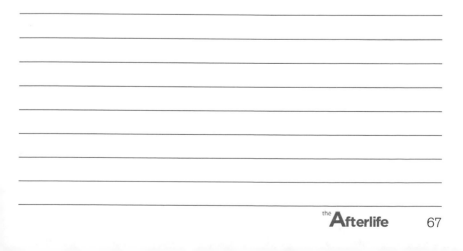

4. HEAVEN IS PERFECT PLEASURE

In heaven, all things are made new. Therefore, it will be a place of perfect pleasure.

> *And He will wipe away every tear from their eyes, and there will be no longer any death and there will no longer be any mourning, or crying, or pain, the first things have passed away. And He who sits on the throne said, Behold, I am making all things new.*
>
> *Revelation 21:4-5*

We all get excited with something new, don't we? We get a gift on our birthday or we buy a new house or we get a new car, and there is an excitement that comes from having something that is new. The problem is, that excitement wears off.

In our eternal state, there will never be a time when sadness shows up because something got old. I will never get used to you, and you will never get used to me. That's what makes heaven exciting. Heaven will never get old.

There is no death, so we will feel brand-new every time the day starts. There is no night there, so all day, every day, we will feel like a brand-new person. So no death, no crying, no tears. You don't even get sad enough to cry, and God is going to wipe away all of our old tears.

How does God help us handle the tears while we are still living on this earth? Read Romans 8:28-31; I Corinthians 10:13; and I Peter 1:6-7 before answering.

_____

_____

_____

_____

_____

_____

_____

_____

5. HEAVEN IS PERFECT KNOWLEDGE

There will be no more turning away from God, we will be turning to Him for all eternity. Every place we run, we will run into God. Everywhere we go, we will run into God. Heaven will be the uninterrupted knowledge of God.

Revelation 22:4 says, "They will see His face, and His name will be on their foreheads." And 1 Corinthians 13:12 says, "For now we see in a mirror dimly, but then face to face; now I know in part, but then I will know fully just as I also have been fully known."

There will be no more secrets. There will be nothing that we cannot discover, because our capacity for knowledge will be

> There will be no more turning away from God, but we will be turning to Him for all eternity. Every place we go, we will run into God. Heaven will be the uninterrupted knowledge of God.

so different from what we have now. The secrets of God will become unveiled to us, and we will be known as we are known.

> Not only will I know things, but I will know you. And you will know me. In fact, we really won't know each other until we get there.

Now, how are we known? God knows us completely. How will we know? We will have the capacity of complete knowledge throughout eternity. Why eternity? God is infinite. There is no end to Him. There will never be an end to our learning. There will never be any knowledge blocks. We will never forget. Our learning will never be hampered.

Why? Because we will see His face. We will look at His face, and there won't be any shadows. There won't be any fog.

And not only will I know *things,* but I will know *you.* And you will know *me.* In fact, we really won't know each other *until* we get there.

What value did Paul place on the true knowledge of Jesus Christ? Read Ephesians 1:15-17, then record your answer.

_____

_____

_____

_____

_____

_____

_____

_____

_____

What questions do you have about God? What will be the first thing you'll want to know when you get to heaven?

_____

_____

_____

_____

_____

_____

_____

_____

_____

6. HEAVEN IS PERFECT LIFE

Nothing will be less than perfect in heaven. It will be perfect life for all who are present.

> Then he showed me a river of the water of life, clear as crystal, coming from the throne of God and of the Lamb, in the middle of its street. On either side of the river was the tree of life, bearing twelve kinds of fruit, yielding its fruit every month; and the leaves of the tree were for the healing of the nations.
>
> _Revelation 22:1-2_

Life will be perfect. We will not want for anything whatsoever. In Matthew 22:23-32, the leaders of Jesus' day were trying to trap Him. Their question: If a woman gets married, her husband dies, she gets married seven other times, her seven other husbands die, and then she dies, who is her husband in the resurrection? Jesus' answer: None of them. "For in the resurrection they neither marry nor are given in marriage, but are like angels in heaven" (v. 30).

We won't *be* angels, but we will be *like* angels. We will be different than angels because we will have glorified bodies, but we will be like the angels in that we will not continue with the same human relationships we have had here on earth. There will be no need for the things those relationships give us.

Adam was given a helper because he needed help. But we husbands won't need help in heaven. A husband is to be his wife's security here on earth, but our wives won't need that security in heaven because they will never feel insecure.

Adam was given a helper because he needed help. But we husbands won't need help in heaven. A husband is to be his wife's security here on earth, but our lives won't need that security in heaven because they will never feel insecure.

We have mates because we need companions, but we will never feel what it's like to be alone in heaven. We have families today, and we have children; when the church is together in heaven, there will be no need for procreation.

The experience of physical intimacy will even be so overshadowed by the experiences of God's divine presence that our earthly intimacy will pale in insignificance when compared to the delight of being thrilled every moment of every day. There will be no need for these things, because for the believer, there will be nothing but uninterrupted, pulsating life.

First John 3:2 says, "We know that when He appears, we will be like Him, because we will see Him just as He is." This verse tells us what our bodies are going to be like.

Christ did some remarkable things after He rose from the dead. He walked through doors when they were closed. So we will have the ability in our glorified bodies to do the same. Our bodies will look like our current bodies, and we'll be the same race we are now, but we will be constructed differently. We will be flawless, and we will be able to walk straight through a wall or a door.

We will also be able to recognize each other in heaven. Mary recognized Jesus when she got a close look at Him. Peter recognized Moses and Elijah when Jesus took him to the Mount of Transfiguration. So we will be able to recognize them. We will know each other because we will look the same as we did before (just without any flaws), plus our knowledge will be so much greater than it is now.

Now, let's look at something that is very, very interesting to me. In Revelation 22:2, there is in this city a boulevard of trees that are lining a crystal-clear aqueduct (v. 1). God's throne is at the top of the city—1,500 miles up-and the water is running down, so gravity exists in this city. Vegetation exists because we see all the trees. And the fruit of the trees changes every month, so there are seasons in this city. All the seasons are good, though, because the fruit keeps changing. So this city includes geology, geography, and all these trees that are full of leaves.

> There will be no need for earthly things, because for the believer, there will be nothing but uninterrupted pulsating life.

Now, why are there leaves on the trees? Verse 2 says they are for the healing of the nations. You may be saying, "But I thought there was no death in heaven. And if there's no death, then how can we ever be sick? Why do we need leaves that produce health and well-being and healing if we can never get sick in the first place?"

If you're asking these questions, you're on the right track. We will already have eternal life, yet this tree gives life. We will already have perfect health, yet this tree makes people healthy.

Now, for the curve ball:

> *The nations will walk by its light, and the kings of the earth will bring their glory into it. In the daytime (for there will be no night there) its gates will never be closed; and they will bring the glory and the honor of the nations into it; and nothing unclean, and no one who practices abomination and lying, shall ever come into it, but only those whose names are written in the Lamb's book of life.*
>
> *Revelation 21:24-27*

This heavenly city includes geology, geography, and all these trees that are full of leaves.

There's another group of people here. These are people who are on this new earth but who do not live in the city. Now, we know that Old Testament saints and the New Testament church live in the city. But here we see kings coming in and out of the city, bringing glory *into* it. Now, if they are bringing glory into it, then there must be glory *outside* of it.

These people are bringing glory and paying homage to God, and they're kings. And in order to have kings, there have to be kingdoms. And if there are kings, there must be people who are being ruled over.

Only the Old Testament saints and New Testament church live inside the city, but there are many people who will come and visit. These people can only fall into one other category than what we have already seen-the group of people from the millennium.

After the tribulation period, Jesus Christ will reign on this earth for 1,000 years. This reign is known as the millennia reign of Christ. During this reign, there will be human beings living on this earth. Then, at the end of the millennium, everyone who did not follow Jesus Christ will be cast into eternal fire.

The rest of the people, the ones who followed Christ, will march into eternity. These people do not receive glorified bodies, but they depend on the tree of life for their healing. Perfect life will be available for everyone.

Read Luke 24:36-43. What limitations are there on Jesus' resurrected, glorified body?

_____

_____

_____

_____

_____

_____

_____

_____

The following Scriptures are the only references to the tree of life in the Bible: Genesis 2:9; 3:22, 24; and Revelation 2:7; 22:2, 14, 19. Make a list of everything you learn.

_____

_____

_____

_____

_____

_____

6. HEAVEN IS PERFECT SERVICE

Finally, heaven will be a place of perfect service. Look at Revelation 22:3-5:

> *There will no longer be any curse; and the throne of God and of the Lamb will be in it, and His bondservants will serve Him; they will see His face, and His name will be on their foreheads. And there will no longer be any night; and they will not have need of the light of a lamp nor the light of the sun, because the Lord God will illumine them; and they will reign forever and ever.*

We will serve Him for all eternity. We will be His priests. If there are kings and kingdoms, then there is organization, there is structure, and there is a whole operation. We are not going to be bored, but we are going to be serving God managing the universe.

Only the Old Testament saints and New Testament church live inside the city, but there are many people who will come and visit.

We will have work to do, but it will be productive. Do you know why you hate to go to work? One of three reasons: You're tired; you don't like it; or you're not getting paid enough.

In heaven, these things won't be a problem. In fact, work and service will be the most fulfilling thing we have to do, and we will be priests to the Lord.

What did servant-minded Paul gladly call himself? Read Ephesians 3:1 and Philemon 1:1, 9, then record your answer.

_____

_____

_____

_____

_____

_____

_____

_____

_____

_____

_____

_____

What does the Bible say about our freedom in Christ? Read Romans 6:16-19 and John 8:34-36.

_____

_____

_____

_____

_____

_____

_____

_____

_____

_____

_____

The fictional character Cinderella had a wicked mother and wicked sister and only through a miracle was she able to go to the ball.

While at the ball, she met the prince. And when she met him it was love at first sight. The only problem was that when midnight came her past caught up with her and she had to return to the real world. But she never forgot the prince, and the prince never forgot her.

Finally, the prince began to search for Cinderella. She was already back with her wicked stepmother and wicked sisters who were trying to make her feel less than what she knew she was. You see once she met the prince, she knew she was a princess.

And even though she was scrubbing the floor and ironing the clothes, she knew she was a princess because she had met the prince.

One day, when you accepted Jesus Christ, you met your prince. But right now you're living with a wicked stepmother named the devil and wicked sisters called demons, and they keep telling you that you're nobody.

Look up, brother. Look up, sister. One day soon your Prince is going to come for you. He is going to break heaven open and call us home, and then we will be with Him forever ... happily ever after.

NOTES

L E S S O N   4
WHAT IS HELL?

Then He will also say...

to those on His left, 'Depart from Me, accursed ones, into the eternal fire which has been prepared for the devil and his angels....'

The Bible gives us a glorious glimpse into what awaits all those who have believed on the Lord Jesus Christ. But for others, the afterlife holds the promise of an eternal hell.

Jesus talked about hell more than He talked about heaven, so if we cannot trust what He said about hell, how can we trust what He promised us about heaven?

Though hell is not a popular topic, it is necessary for two reasons. First, Christians need to have an understanding of what Christ has saved us *from*. Second, non-Christians need to have an understanding of *why* they need to be saved from it.

Most people live in a state of denial about hell. While 76 percent of Americans believe in heaven, only 6 percent believe in hell. In fact, many people have developed what we might call coping mechanisms to try to deal with this subject.

Some people try to cope by denying the existence of hell. Others try to cope by adopting a belief in annihilation, where there is no afterlife but everything is destroyed. Still others try to cope by taking the position that someway, somehow, God is going to save everybody.

> We can know that hell is real because the Bible says it is, Jesus says it is, and the apostles say it is. But we can also know that hell is real because death is real. And death exists because of sin.

At the heart of all this is a viewpoint that says if God exists and is a God of love, then there cannot be a place called hell. We must allow God to speak for Himself. He does not need us to speak for Him.

As we approach this most serious subject, it is crucial for us to understand that our reasoning must be subject to God's revelation. No amount of dismissing it can remove it from God's Word.

1. THE REALITY OF HELL

Hell is the place of eternal exile where the ungodly experience God's just retribution against sin. And it is as real as real can get.

> *"Then He will also say to those on His left, Depart from Me, accursed ones, into the eternal fire which has been prepared for the devil and his angels. ... These will go away into eternal punishment, but the righteous into eternal life."*
>
> Matthew 25:41,46

There are two things that we must not miss as we begin this part of our study and before we catch a glimpse of hell. First, the reality of eternal fire is recorded for us in the Bible. The idea of hell does not come from extra-biblical sources but from the very Word of God.

Second, these words from Matthew 25 are words that were spoken by the Lord Jesus Christ Himself. Therefore, if hell is not real, then the Bible is not trustworthy. And if hell is not real, then Jesus is not trustworthy.

Jesus talked about hell more than He talked about heaven, so if we cannot trust what He said about hell, how can we trust what He promised us about heaven? If we can't accept the reality of the bad stuff, how can we put our confidence in Him when He talks about the good stuff?

In Matthew 25:46, the word *eternal* is used twice as "eternal punishment" and "eternal life." It's the same Greek word. So do not trick yourself into thinking, "Heaven is eternal life, but hell is not necessarily eternal." If heaven lasts forever, hell lasts forever.

If hell does not last forever, then how do we know that heaven will last forever? In fact, the Bible says that God is eternal. If hell comes to an end, perhaps heaven will come to an end. God might even come to an end, for the word *eternal* is used to describe heaven, hell, and God. There is much more at stake for those who deny the reality of hell.

> Hell exists for the purpose of being the eternal place of exile for Satan and his angels.

It is because hell is real that Jesus spent so much time warning people about it.

> *"If your hand or your foot causes you to stumble cut it off and throw it from you; it is better for you to enter life crippled or lame than to have two hands or two feet and be cast into the eternal fire. If your eye causes you to stumble pluck it out and throw it from you. It is better for you to enter life with one eye than to have two eyes and be cast into the fire of hell."*
>
> Matthew 18:8-9

LESSON 4

> Hell was never created with human beings in mind. It was created for the devil and his demons.

He wants us to avoid this place at all costs. The dangers of being lured by sin are very real. If there is something you choose to do (your hand), somewhere you choose to go (your feet), or something you choose to look at (your eyes) that might become an avenue that would lead you into hell, get rid of it. It is better to be deformed on earth than to be lost for eternity in hell.

We can know that hell is real because the Bible says it is, Jesus says it is, and the apostles say it is. But we can also know that hell is real because death is real. And death exists because of sin. If there were no sin, there would be no death. Death is the temporal reality of sin, and hell is the eternal reality of the presence of sin. That's why it is called the second death.

Read John 3:16, 36. How does God show us that there are only two choices?

_____

_____

_____

_____

_____

_____

_____

_____

_____

_____

_____

Read John 8:43, 47. What does Jesus say about the person who rejects His Word?

_____

_____

_____

_____

_____

_____

_____

_____

2. THE RESIDENTS OF HELL

So who belongs in hell? Matthew 25:41 says the eternal fire "has been prepared for the devil and his angels." Hell exists for the purpose of being in the eternal place of exile for Satan and his angels.

Now, why are Satan and his angels destined for this eternal fire? They will spend eternity here because a long, long time ago, they made a choice to live independently of God.

Ezekiel 28 and Isaiah 14 give us the account of when Satan chose to rebel against the Most High God. He decided to be his own master, the captain of his own ship, the god of his own faith, with no one to rule over him. He was a creature rebelling against his Creator, and the creature lost. God pre-

> When a person rejects God and chooses to follow Satan instead, God will not interfere. If you love the devil that much, then God will let you live with him forever.

pared this place of eternal fire so that Satan and his angels would be eternally reminded of the consequences of spiritual rebellion.

> You were created to be eternal, and you were created in the very image of God. That makes you and your choices very significant.

Hell was never created with human beings in mind. It was created for the devil and his demons. Eternal separation from God was their own choice.

Satan and his angels are not the only ones in hell, though. There are many, many people who will be in hell. These people go to hell, which was not prepared for people, because they make the same choice as Satan and his angels.

You cannot go to hell by chance; you can only go to hell by choice. Everybody who is in hell chose to go there, because the decision to go to hell is built into the decision to reject God. In other words, to reject God is to go to hell. You don't have to say, "I want to go to hell." You only have to say, "I don't want You, God." Hell is the answer to the sinner's prayer.

The book of Revelation sheds more light on the matter of choice:

> *Then another angel, a third one, followed them saying with a loud voice, 'if anyone worships the beast and his image and receives a mark on his forehead or on his hand, he also will drink of the wine of the wrath of God, which is mixed in full strength in the cup of His anger; and he will be tormented with fire and brimstone in the presence of the holy angels and in the presence of the Lamb. And the smoke of their torment goes up forever and ever; they have no*

*rest day and night those who worship the beast and his image and
whoever receives the mark of his name."*

Revelation 14:9-11

The beast and false prophet are going to be there, too. And they will be joined
by those who choose to receive the mark of the beast. When a person rejects
God and chooses to follow Satan instead, God will not interfere. If you love
the devil that much, then God will let you live with him forever.

A man was on an airplane one day, and he was talking with another man
who happened to be a preacher. The man asked, "Preacher, do you believe
in hell?" The preacher said, "Well, yes." The man said, "I can't believe that.
Why?" The preacher's answer was simple yet profound. He said, "Man was
created uniquely significant, because he was created in the image of God."

Because man is significant, so are his choices. If there were no hell, you
would not be significant. But you were created to be eternal, and you were
created in the very image of God. That makes you and your choices very
significant.

> At the very core of this issue of hell is the
> character of God. We often fail to see
> that God has two sides, not just one.

*"But for the cowardly and unbelieving and abominable and murder-
ers and immoral persons and sorcerers and idolaters and all liars,
their part will be in the lake that burns with fire and brimstone which
is the second death. . . . Outside are the dogs and the sorcerers
and the immoral persons and the murderers and the idolaters, and
everyone who loves and practices lying."*

Revelation 21:8; 22:15

LESSON 4

Hell was prepared for the devil and his angels, but the wicked go there by choice. Now, I'm sure you have heard this common complaint: "I don't believe God would send people to hell." First, He doesn't send them; hell is a choice they make for themselves. Second, hell is not for a generic group of people, but its residents are specifically unsaved sinners.

What are some of the choices that are made by the residents of the eternal fire? Read Isaiah 14:12-15; Ezekiel 28:11-19; Revelation 13:1-8, 11-17; and 20:12, then record your answer.

_____

_____

_____

_____

_____

_____

_____

Read Matthew 5:20; 7:21; and 1Corinthians 6:9-10. Where are you standing in relation to the afterlife? Are you headed toward eternal life in heaven or eternal fire in hell?

_____

_____

_____

_____

_____

_____

3. THE REASON FOR HELL

Before we can truly comprehend what hell is, we must understand the reason for hell. Why does it exist? Look at Romans 1:18: "For the wrath of God is revealed from heaven against all ungodliness and unrighteousness of men who suppress the truth in unrighteousness."

At the very core of this issue of hell is the character of God. We often fail to see that God has two sides, not just one. Romans 11:22 says, "Behold then the kindness and severity of God; to those who fell, severity; but to you, God's kindness, if you continue in His kindness; otherwise, you also will be cut off."

So God is both kind and severe. Don't ever focus on His love to the extent that you neglect His righteousness or His justice. Yes, God is love. But God is also holy. His eyes are too pure to even look on evil (Habakkuk 1:13). Because God is just, He must deal with sin (Nahum 1:2-3).

God cannot overlook sin, because that would be contrary to His nature. He must respond to sin in our lives because we were made in His image. Therefore, God's wrath is His righteous retribution against us.

> God cannot over-look sin because that would be contrary to His nature. He must respond to sin in our lives because we were made in His image.

God's wrath can be either passive or active. His passive wrath is evident in Romans 1. In verse 21, men did not honor Him as God. Therefore, in verse 24, God gave them over in the lusts of their hearts to impurity; in verse 26, God gave them over to degrading passions. In verse 28, they did not see fit to acknowledge God any longer, so He gave them over to a depraved mind.

These verses show God's passive wrath. In other words, He simply stepped out of the way and allowed sin and evil to take their course. He withdraws His protection at this point and allows Satan free reign.

God's wrath can also be active, as we see in Romans 2:5: "But because of your stubbornness and unrepentant heart you are storing up wrath for yourself in the day of wrath and revelation of the righteous judgment of God." In this day, God is going to pounce.

Parents demonstrate passive wrath when we say to our kids, "Because of the way you're acting, there will be no pizza for you." Active wrath, however, is saying, "All right. That's it. You are grounded."

God is too holy to look at sin and therefore cannot spend eternity with the sinner. So the only logical place for the sinner is hell. But be warned, "It is a terrifying thing to fall into the hands of the living God" (Hebrews 10:31).

The afterlife offers no second chances. Is this really fair? Read Luke 16:27-31, then record your answer.

_____

_____

_____

_____

_____

_____

_____

_____

_____

_____

Read Romans 1:18-32. What begins to happen when a person rejects God?

_____

_____

_____

_____

_____

_____

_____

_____

_____

_____

4. THE REALM OF GOD

The Greek word for "hell" that Jesus regularly used in the Gospels is *Gehenna*. I have had the opportunity to go to Israel, and I have looked in the place called Gehenna.

> "It is a terrifying thing to fall into the hands of the living God." Hebrews 10:31

In New Testament days, Gehenna was the local garbage dump outside of Jerusalem. People would dump their garbage there and then set it on fire in order to burn it up.

Also, this was a burial place for wicked people. If you were a criminal, you couldn't be buried at a decent burial site; instead, you were buried in Gehenna.

The Bible also speaks of Gehenna as a place where the worm never dies. That's because this garbage dump bred worms. And no matter how many flames there were to burn up the garbage, the worms always remained-because they feed on filth. Can you see the connection? Hell is a wasteland outside of God's goodness where there is no exit and no change.

> *And the devil who deceived them was thrown into the lake of fire and brimstone where the beast and the false prophet are also; and they will be tormented day and night forever and ever. Then I saw a great white throne and Him who sat upon it from whose presence earth and heaven fled away and no place was found for them. And I saw the dead the great and the small standing before the throne and books were opened; and another book was opened which is the book of life; and the dead were from the things which were written in the books according to their deeds. And the sea gave up the dead"*

Hell is a wasteland outside of God's goodness where there is no exit and no change.

What was cast into the lake of fire? Death and Hades were thrown into the lake of fire (v. 14). We often talk about "hell" more than we do "the lake of fire," but hell is only a temporary place. When a non-believer dies, he immediately goes to hell. At the final judgment, hell will be thrown into the lake of fire. The lake of fire is the final, permanent home of sinners.

The best illustration of hell that I know is Alcatraz, which is located right outside the city of San Francisco. Alcatraz is a place of exile. Though it is more of a museum now, it used to be the place criminals were sent to be incarcerated for their crimes.

Situated around Alcatraz is a body of water that is shark-infested. So anyone trying to escape from Alcatraz faced two problems: one, if you try to swim, you'll drown before you reach San Francisco. Two, if you try to swim, a shark will eat you before you reach San Francisco.

> At the final judgment, hell will be thrown into the lake of fire. The lake of fire is the final permanent home of sinners.

The body of water that surrounds the prison was a guarantee that nobody would escape from the facility. That water was so infested that nobody could go anywhere. In the same way, hell is the prison where all the ungodly people go who do not have eternal life abiding within them. It is the place that has been constructed for Satan and his angels; they will dwell there, along with those who have chosen to side with them in rebellion against God.

Now, in most prisons, not everyone is equal. Some of the prisoners are under maximum security, some are under medium security, and others are under minimal security. The punishment depends on the severity of the crime committed.

Hell, or the lake of fire, will be the same way. The Bible tells us that not all people are going to be equal. The worst sinners will go to a sort of maximum-security area. The mediocre sinners will go to a sort of medium-security area. And the nice sinners who committed a few mental sins but really didn't do too many things that were just really, really bad will go to a sort of minimum-security area. However, they're all going to spend eternity in the same place, a "spiritual Alcatraz."

When people think of hell, they think of fire and flames and heat. If you'll look back at the rich man in Luke 16, he wasn't screaming from the midst of fiery flames; he was having an intelligent conversation. So what was the torment? Without a doubt, the worst torment of all is this: You can stand on Alcatraz

> The worst part of hell, the worst part of the lake of fire, is being able to see heaven from a distance but not being able to go there.

and see San Francisco in the distance. And the rich man opened his eyes and saw Lazarus from a distance.

From Alcatraz, you can see the tall buildings; the high rises, the pulsating life in the big city. But all you can do is look at what could have been and what will never be. The worst part of hell, the worst part of the lake of fire, is being able to see heaven from a distance but not being able to go there. It is surrounded by fire and brimstone, and you can't get out. There's no escaping this place. It might not be as bad for the nice sinners as it is for the not so-nice sinners, but so what? The unbeliever is still stuck there and can never get to the other side. How terribly sad.

Did you know that the lake of fire offers different degrees of punishment for the wicked? Read the following verses and note what you find.

_____

_____

_____

_____

_____

_____

Matthew 10:21-24:

_____

_____

_____

_____

_____

_____

Matthew 12:38-42:

_____

_____

_____

_____

_____

_____

Luke 10:10-16:

_____

_____

_____

_____

_____

"I'm not a bad person. I've never stolen anything. I've never murdered anybody. I don't need to be saved." What would you say to this person?

_____

_____

_____

_____

_____

_____

_____

_____

5. THE RESCUE FROM HELL

Have you rejected the Lord Jesus Christ? Hell is waiting. The door's open. Satan's calling. Are you ready to go?

If not, there's good news. God wants to offer you a substitute for hell. And He wants you to accept His offer.

Did you know that there is only one reason that Jesus Christ has not returned to this earth yet? Second Peter 3:9 says, "The Lord is not slow about His promise, as some count slowness, but is patient toward you, not wishing for any to perish but for all to come to repentance." He's waiting for just a few more to come to Him!

> God wants to offer you a substitute for hell. And He wants you to accept His offer.

What is God's substitute program like? Because God cannot compromise His nature and skip over sin, He has to let somebody else die in your place. Are you saying, "Oh, all right. Then I'll just have to find somebody to take my place." It's not that easy.

First, nobody is going to want to take your place. And second, nobody you know is qualified to take your place, because whoever substitutes for you must be an acceptable substitute and therefore not have to go to hell themselves. And the only man who qualifies to be your substitute is the God-Man, the Lord Jesus Christ.

Second Corinthians 5:21 says, "He made Him who knew no sin to be sin on our behalf, so that we might become the righteousness of God in Him." On the cross, God sent Jesus to "Alcatraz" and heaped on Him an eternity's worth of judgment so that He could switch places with you.

Almighty God has offered a substitute program for you, and all you have to do is accept Jesus Christ as that Substitute. The Bible says we must accept that we are sinners and that Jesus is the only way. You can do this by saying, "God, I acknowledge that I am a sinner, and I deserve to go to hell, but I don't want to go there. I want Jesus Christ to be my Substitute. I look to Him alone as the payment for my sin. I place my eternal confidence not in what I can do-because I have already blown it-but in what He has already done."

If you will only come to Him, God will take the blood of Christ and apply it to your account, forgiving you of all your sins and giving you a transfer out of hell and into heaven. This substitute program is God's means of rescuing you and me from a real place, an eternal place, called hell, where the "worm does not die, and the fire is not quenched" (Mark 9:44).

Do you believe Jesus is the only way you can get to heaven in the after-life? What does the Bible say? Read John 14:6, then record your answer.

_____

_____

_____

_____

_____

Read the following passages from the book of Romans. As you read each one, spend some time thinking about your personal relationship with Jesus Christ. Have you experienced what is mentioned in these passages, or do you still need to turn to Jesus as your Substitute?

_____

_____

_____

_____

_____

Romans 3:23:

_____

_____

_____

_____

_____

Romans 6:23:

_____

_____

_____

_____

Romans 10:9-10:

_____

_____

_____

_____

_____

Is God's way of salvation the only way, or is it possible for a person to somehow get to heaven on his own terms as long as he says he is a Christian? Read Matthew 7:21-23, then record your answer.

_____

_____

_____

_____

_____

If you were to die this very moment, where would you spend eternity? The afterlife is a reality, and there are only two choices. If you have not yet made your choice, then spend some time right now just getting quiet before God. This is not a decision you can afford to put off. When you're ready, write down where you will spend eternity ... and why.

_____

_____

_____

_____

_____

The character of God demands that sin cannot go unpunished. If our God, who is holy, righteous, and just, were to overlook sin, He would have to change who He Is. And that's just not possible, "for He cannot deny Himself" (2 Timothy 2:13).

I know most of us would prefer that we just meet together, talking about the love of God and how to make this world a better place, and peace and joy and happiness. But if we forget the other side of God, our picture of who God is will be out of balance.

The other side of God is not the popular side. It's not the side I like preaching about. It's not the side I like talking about. But what kind of a fireman would I be if I didn't warn you about fire? What kind of policeman would I be if I didn't warn you about criminals? What kind of doctor would I be if I didn't warn you about disease? And what kind of pastor would I be if I didn't warn you about hell?

I have done my part. You have been warned. If you're not yet a Christian, won't you come over to our side ... while you still can?

NOTES

LESSON 5
WHAT IS HELL LIKE?

In Hades...

he lifted his eyes, being in torment, and saw Abraham far away and Lazarus in his bosom.

An Army chaplain approached his men during a Sunday morning service and said, "Men, I don't believe in hell."

The man is in agony and torment, yet he has all of his physical faculties. He can see, he can talk, he can feel, and he is begging for a fingertip to bring him some water because of the torment of the flame.

After the service was over, some of the men started talking and realized that if there is no hell, and if death is the only thing left for us to face, then we might as well live as if there are no consequences for our actions.

The men met with the chaplain in private and said, "Sir, your services are no longer needed. If there is no hell, then nothing matters. If there is a hell, then you are leading us astray. Either way, we're better off without you."

One of the ways fire is used in the Bible is as a symbol of God's purifying justice. Therefore, what we have in Luke 16 is a description of a man in a fire environment with no relief available to him.

My friend, there is a place called hell, and I say that to you on the authority of God's Word. We are careful to warn our children about fire, about electric sockets, about snakes, and about cars that come down the middle of the street because we know that these things can cause great pain.

In the same way, I am joining Jesus Christ Himself to warn you about the reality of an eternity separated from Christ. The Bible calls this place hell.

When we step into the afterlife, we step into eternity. When we step into the afterlife, our choice has already been made. When we step into the afterlife, reality kicks in.

In Luke 16, the rich man died and woke up in Hades. It was the first day of the rest of his life, and the Bible says he "lifted up his eyes, being in torment" (v. 23).

1. HELL IS A PLACE OF PHYSICAL TORMENT

The person who wakes up in hell can kiss comfort goodbye, for this place is a place of physical torment.

> ''In Hades he lifted up his eyes, being in torment, and saw Abraham far away and Lazarus in his bosom. And he cried out and said, Father Abraham, have mercy on me, and send Lazarus so that he may dip the tip of his finger in water and cool off my tongue, for I am in agony in this flame.''
>
> Luke 16:23-24

Verse 23 says, "he lifted up his eyes." Verse 24 says, "he cried out and said." At the end of verse 24, he says, "Cool off my tongue." In other words, he is there in physical form. Now, a person's soul, or spiritual form, immediately goes to hell; there is no physical form until after the resurrection. But, eventually, those in hell will receive physical bodies just as the saints in heaven will receive new bodies.

Because Jesus was speaking in terms of the physical body, I believe what He was doing was giving an early warning about the eternal state, which is described in more detail at the end of the book of Revelation.

But we see in this picture that the man is in agony and torment, yet he has all of his physical faculties. He can see, he can talk, he can feel, and he is begging for a fingertip to bring him some water because of the torment of the flame.

> I cannot even imagine what it will be like for those on whom God will unleash His complete wrath, nor do I wish to imagine an abyss where you just keep falling, falling, falling into more and more misery.

I contend that this is not a description of physical bodies that are literally on fire. I do not believe that this is a picture of people who are experiencing flames bursting out of their flesh. The Bible says there is a flame, but I believe that flame is the environment that surrounds the people who live there.

Notice that when this man speaks, he doesn't wake up and start screaming or shouting. He begins to engage in an intelligent conversation. He is somewhat logical, he can interact with another person, and yet he is in agony. His request is not to be doused in water; he only wants a drop on his tongue. So this man can function physically, although in agony.

> And, just as in heaven, where there is never any night, in hell there will never be another sunrise.

The best illustration of this concept, I believe, is a man living in the Sahara Desert. The sun beats down on him 24 hours a day at about 200 degrees Fahrenheit, and there is no relief available-no iced tea, no water, no refreshments. He can still function-he can communicate, he can think logically, and he can do all the normal things that people do-but he is stilling in an inflamed environment.

I live in Texas, and frequently during the summer the temperature will reach 110 or 112 degrees. It's next to impossible to be outside for a couple of minutes without perspiring or sweating, and I can't imagine what it would be like without air conditioning.

This kind of heat, this kind of agony, is nothing compared to what hell is like. One of the ways fire is used in the Bible is as a symbol of God's purifying justice. Therefore, what we have in Luke 16 is a description of a man in a fire environment with no relief available to him. This is a miserable existence.

The Bible also calls this place "the bottomless pit" and "the abyss" (Revelation 9:1-2; 11:7; 17:8). The concept of the abyss is an immeasurable place where things only get worse and worse and worse. The terrible thing about hell is that wherever you turn, you cannot escape the misery-because you are forever separated from the presence of God.

The rich man in Luke 16 opens his eyes and immediately finds himself in torment. Now, you and I have witnessed a very little portion of the wrath of God. We have only seen His wrath in miniscule form, because His full wrath is being held back at this time by His other attributes, such as mercy.
I cannot even imagine what it will be like for those on whom God will unleash His complete wrath, nor do I wish to imagine an abyss where you just keep falling, falling, falling into more and more misery.

And, just as in heaven, where there is never any night, in hell there will never be another sunrise. It will always be night there (see Jude 13). This is eternal darkness, and the only light will be that light that comes from the lava of the lake of fire. This is the most you can expect from a world where God only expresses His wrath—because His justice demands it.

Is the wrath of God a new concept for you? Read the following verses, then note what you learn about God's wrath: Revelation 6:16-17; 11:18; 14:10, 19; 15:1, 7; 16:1,19; and 19:15.

_____

_____

_____

_____

_____

_____

_____

_____

_____

Read Romans 8:1. If all have sinned, how is it that Christians have escaped the wrath and condemnation of God? Now read 2 Corinthians 5:21, then record your answer.

_____

_____

_____

_____

_____

_____

_____

2. HELL IS A PLACE OF SOCIAL TORMENT

Luke 16:23 says, "In Hades he lifted up his eyes, being in torment, and saw Abraham far away and Lazarus in his bosom."

> A person is in hell, surrounded by the lake of fire. Then he looks up and catches a glimpse of heaven. Can you imagine having to accept hell as your eternal home while at the same time acknowledging the wonders of heaven?

Now, I am suggesting that Jesus has given us a picture of what hell will be like after it is cast into the lake of fire, because this is when the residents of hell will have their resurrected bodies.

This is a place of social torment. As the rich man looks up, he sees Abraham ... far away. He sees Lazarus ... in Abraham's bosom. In our last lesson, I used the illustration of Alcatraz. Prisoners who lived on Alcatraz Island could see the city of San Francisco from a distance, but they could never go there.

Just think about it. A person is in hell, surrounded by the lake of fire. Then he looks up and catches a glimpse of heaven. Can you imagine having to accept hell as your eternal home while at the same time acknowledging the wonders of heaven, which you will never see or enjoy or experience for yourself? Hell is an eternal reminder to its residents that they rejected God's free gift of salvation.

A popular singer once said, "I can't wait to go to hell so I can be with all my homies." Proverbs 11:7 says, "When a wicked man dies, his expectation will perish, and the hope of strong men perishes." Your "homies" may be there, but they won't be there to offer sympathy, because hell isn't the big party you've heard about. Keep this in mind:

"Then they will go forth and look on the corpses of the men who have transgressed against Me. For their worm will not die and their fire will not be quenched; and they will be an abhorrence to all mankind."

Isaiah 66:24

The Bible says that everyone who lives in hell will be an abhorrence to every other person who lives in hell. The party got called off. The "homies" won't be hanging out together. In fact, there won't be any "homies" there.

There will be other people in hell, but those people won't be offering their sympathy. You and your former friends will see each other as a disgrace. Gehenna was a garbage dump that was full of maggots. It was a place of disgrace, it had a stench, and it was nasty.

If you were to walk by that dump, you would have to hold your nose and say, "Yuck!" It would just be agonizing to even look at it. You know how repulsive it is to look at rotten garbage. You know what it looks like and what it smells like. I believe this is what hell is like.

I believe you'll see someone coming, and you'll turn your head. They ·will look terrible, they will smell terrible, and you cannot even stand to be around anybody else.

People will also be hateful to each other in hell. Every time one person runs into another person, the two will not be able to get along. Do you know why? Because in hell, the sin nature of mankind will have its fullest expression.

> The Bible says that everyone who lives in hell will be an abhorrence to every other person who lives in hell. The party got called off.

In hell, everybody will be able to fully express who they are apart from redemption. Therefore, everybody will be repulsed by everybody else. The sin nature will make everybody look so bad to everybody else that, no matter how many people are there, each individual will, in a sense, remain in his own solitary confinement. That's why Jesus calls it the second death.

> There will be no negative remembrances for believers who go to heaven about anything in hell, but there will be eternal regret in hell for people who missed heaven.

What is death? Death is separation. Those who go to hell will not only be separated from the experience of God's love, but they will also be separated from everybody else. It is not a pleasant picture.

Someone has asked me, "Will we see people in hell, and how can we stand to be in heaven when our loved ones who didn't become Christians are suffering in hell?" The Bible says that in heaven, the former things will be remembered no more. There will be no negative remembrances for believers who go to heaven about anything in hell, but there will be eternal regret in hell for people who missed heaven. Hell is a place of social torment.

"I might as well go to hell. That's where all my friends are." Based on what you have read, how should you respond to such a statement?

_____

_____

_____

_____

_____

_____

_____

_____

_____

_____

There won't be any socializing in hell. Who would you never see again if you were to go to hell today? Who would you never see again if you were to go to heaven today?

_____

_____

_____

_____

_____

_____

_____

_____

3. HELL IS A PLACE OF PSYCHOLOGICAL TORMENT

The next aspect of hell-its psychological torment-is hard to think about. This torment will exist because people in hell will still remember the former things.

In Luke 16:25, when Abraham answered the cry of the rich man, he started out by saying, "Child, remember…" Are there mistakes, errors, or regrets that you want to forget about? Are there things you would have or should have done differently? Those who choose hell as their eternal home will have all eternity to ponder the failures of the past.

Now, let's take another look at the work that we have mentioned before.

If your hand causes you to stumble, cut it off; it is better for you to enter life crippled than having your two hands to go into hell into the unquenchable fire where their worm does not die and the fire is not quenched.

Mark 9:43-48

Then the phrase is repeated in verse 48: "where their worm does not die, and the fire is not quenched." In other words, the fire never goes out. The flame never dies. This environment is eternal.

We have already seen this worm mentioned in Isaiah 66, but I want to give you two more facts about it. First, the word *worm* is singular. It does not say "where their worms do not die," but "where their worm does not die."

Second, it is not "the worm." It is "their worm." It is a personalized worm. This raises the question, What is their worm? The fire tells us about the external retribution-the surrounding environment. I believe that the worm, because it is not "the" worm and because it is singular, refers to the internal environment. That is, if you are in hell, then the worm is you living with you.

Physiological torment will exist because people in hell will still remember the former things.

When Abraham says, "remember," I believe he is referring to that worm, which will gnaw on you like maggots on a carcass in that old dump called Gehenna. I believe you will remember that Sunday in church when that preacher told you about hell and you didn't pay attention. I believe you'll remember that day as if it were only yesterday.

I believe you'll remember that maybe you were even a member of that church, yet you kept putting off the decision you kept hearing so much about. The preacher talked about hell and you laughed. The preacher talked about eternity, and you laughed. The preacher talked about your soul, and you laughed. But then came death, then came the afterlife, and you're not laughing anymore.

Those who live in hell will have an eternity to remember that it did not have to be this way. What did Abraham say? "Child, remember that during your life you received your good things, and likewise Lazarus bad things; but now he is being comforted here, and you are in agony" (Luke 16:25). Everything is reversed in hell. It is the ultimate reversal of fortune.

> When Abraham says "remember," I believe he is referring to the worm, which will gnaw on you like maggots on a carcass in that old dump called Gehenna.

That reversal is on an individual level. While the external environment may be the same for everybody, the internal retribution is your own. This is why there are different degrees of punishment in hell.

How will the degree of punishment be decided? By your works. See, works do not determine whether or not a person goes to heaven, because a person doesn't go to heaven because of his works. But the wicked are judged according to their works, or their deeds.

In this life, many sinful desires go unfulfilled. Consider the drug addicts who can't get any drugs. They're miserable men and women. They go to the crack house, and nobody's home. So they go through withdrawals and start sweating and trembling and shaking because their passion has gone unfulfilled. Consider the alcoholic who can't get any alcohol. Think about the sex addict

> You know how it is when you want to sin. Nobody else knows you want to sin, but you are burning up inside because you want to sin so bad. You want to sin so bad that you can't sleep.

who can't get enough sex. Sin's burning desires sometimes go unfulfilled.

However, in hell, that sin nature will be set free from all restraint. And that sin nature will be totally unleashed. There won't be any distractions like work or parties or television to take your mind off your sinful desires. Yet, even though that nature is unleashed and there is freedom to sin, sin, sin, there will never be satisfaction. No water. Only agony.

You know how it is when you want to sin. Nobody else knows you want to sin, but you are burning up inside because you want to sin so bad. You want to sin so bad that you can't sleep.

That burning feeling, that gnawing feeling, will be permanent in hell. It will last day in and day out. Have you ever been in bed at night when the faucet started dripping? Blop ... blop... blop ... blop ... blop ... blop ... blop.

You finally got out of bed, tried to fix it, and went back to bed. Drip ... drip ... drip ... drip . . . drip . . . drip . . . drip . . . drip . . .drip. You pulled the pillow over your head, but it got louder and louder and louder.

Or maybe you have been around people who just talk ... talk ... talk ... talk. . . talk . . . talk . . . talk . . . talk . . . talk . . . talk. You try to be nice, but they won't stop. It gets to you, doesn't it? In hell, the nagging noises, the irritating sounds, and all the annoyances of the world will be on center stage ... forever ... and ever ... and ever ... and ever.

There can never be peace in a place that is missing the Prince of Peace. Isaiah 48:22 says, "There is no peace for the wicked."

Not only is there no peace, but there are also no dreams, no goals, no high schools to graduate from, no jobs to take, no civilization, no buildings, no high rises, no construction programs. It's just a marsh, a swamp, a wasteland.

You may have had good things in this life, but every good thing you have ever had came from God (James 1:17). And the goodness of God cannot be found in hell; it's removed from you for all eternity. That's why there is only darkness, nighttime, and nothingness.

"Hell is the ultimate reversal of fortune." Compare this statement with Matthew 6:19–21 and Luke 17:33. How should this affect your life right now?

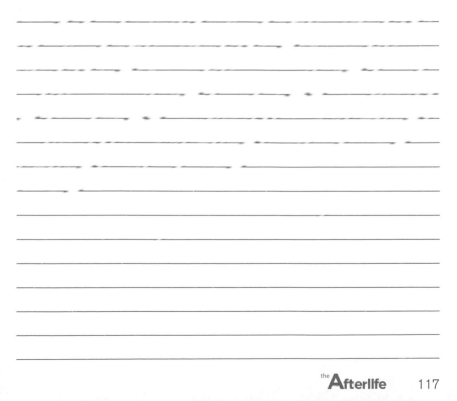

A person's works determine the degree of punishment he will receive in hell. On a scale of 1 to 10 (with 10 being the worst punishment possible), where would your works (or the way you live) place you on that scale?

_____

_____

_____

_____

_____

_____

_____

_____

_____

_____

_____

4. HELL IS A PLACE OF ETERNAL TORMENT

As if the first three points aren't bad enough, hell is a place of eternal torment.

> *"And besides all this, between us and you there is a great chasm fixed so that those who wish to come over from here to you will not be able and that none may cross over from there to us."*
>
> *Luke 16:26*

In Luke 16, Jesus has given us a picture of what hell is like. The Bible says that hell will be cast into the lake of fire. And if a lake of fire surrounds you, then there is no possibility of escape. Revelation 14:11 says "they have no rest day and night."

In hell, there are no seconds or minutes or hours or days or weeks or years or decades or centuries or millennia. Watches don't work there, because there is no time. One hundred billion years and one second are twins.

Nobody ever leaves this place. It is a life sentence, and you live forever. It is like being put in a prison for life, and the only thing you can hope for is death. But, though the fire never goes out, death never comes. This death is eternal.

My friend, if you are not afraid of hell, then the odds are that you'll be spending eternity there. If you do not feel terror today as you read about this place called hell, it could be that you will someday get to experience that terror firsthand.

There are two phrases that I believe are going to be repeated over and over again in hell. The first one is, "Too late." The other one is, "I wish." If you have not made reservations in heaven, then your existence in the afterlife is going to be pure hell. Unless you are reconciled to God through His Son, Jesus Christ, you will live with the most miserable regrets ... for all eternity.

> Works do not determine whether or not a person goes to heaven, because a person doesn't go to heaven because of his works. But the wicked are judged according to their works.

Take a minute and think about the word eternal. Why is it so important to make a decision today concerning Jesus Christ?

_____

_____

_____

_____

_____

_____

_____

_____

**Because eternity is forever, God wants you and those you love to have
every opportunity to believe in Him before you step into the afterlife.
Read 2 Peter 3:9. Where is the balance between the wrath of God and
the mercy of God?**

_____

_____

_____

_____

_____

_____

_____

_____

*Jesus' message to the church in Smyrna, to the other six churches
in Asia, and to every single Christian alive is this: He who has an
ear, let him hear what the Spirit says to the churches. He who
overcomes will not be hurt by the second death-"*
(Revelation 2:11).

*God has come up with a way for you and me to never have to experience hell
and the lake of fire. He has come up with a way for you and me to escape
being hurt by the second death.*

*We never have to know what it's like because God has prepared a cell vaccine.
He has come up with a pardon so that we never have to worry about hell again.*

If you have come to God through faith in Jesus Christ, you have received forgiveness of sins, you have received eternal life, and you can call heaven your eternal home.

If you have come to God through faith in Jesus Christ, you have received forgiveness of sins, you have received eternal life, and you can call heaven your eternal home.

If you have not come to God through faith in Jesus Christ, this is your opportunity. You can pray to God right now, saying,

> "Dear God, I don't want to go to hell. I don't want to spend an eternity separated from You. I accept Your forgiveness of sins offered by Jesus Christ because of His death on the cross, and I look to Him as the Guarantor of my eternal salvation."

God does not want anyone to perish, and that is why He sent Jesus to this earth to die in your place, so that you wouldn't have to die.

NOTES

LESSON 6

WHAT ABOUT THOSE WHO CAN'T BELIEVE?

And Jesus called...

*a child to Himself and set him before them, and said, 'Truly I say to you,
unless you are converted and become like children, you will not enter the
kingdom of heaven.'*

On more than one occasion, a mother has come to me because she had mis-
carried or her baby was stillborn. Her question is always, "Where is my baby?"

The Bible says that all men are
born into sin and shaped in inequity. When we are born, the Bible
says, we are "children of wrath."

There have been occasions when parents of mentally retarded children have
asked, "What is the spiritual status of my child?"

And then there are the numerous occasions when people have come to me
with this question: "What is the spiritual status of those who have never heard
the name of Jesus Christ?"

I could not conclude our study of the afterlife without raising this funda-
mental, controversial, and most difficult question: What about those who
can't believe?

People are always forming these questions in the back of their minds. What about those who can't believe? What about those who do not have either the mental capacity or the available knowledge to respond to the Gospel? What is the hope for such people? *Is* there any hope for such people?

We're going to see the answer in the next several pages. But before we get started, I want to clarify one thing. By "those who can't believe," I am not referring to those who choose not to believe. I am only referring to those who lack the capacity to believe or those who do not have information available to them.

1. THE PROBLEM OF THOSE WHO CAN'T BELIEVE

When many Christians consider the question of what happens to those who can't believe, many are normally thrown out to dry to this difficult issue.

Some people will just say, "Well, a God of love could not send such people to hell." But that kind of reasoning is problematic, because people whom God loves go to hell every day. The love of God does not automatically allow everyone to go to heaven.

> The question we must ask ourselves is, If belief in Christ is necessary for salvation, what happens to people who can't believe?

Others will try to solve this problem by baptizing babies. Some denominations believe that the ritual of baptism will somehow bring a cleansing effect to their children. But the Bible is very clear on the fact that we are not forgiven for our sins by simply being baptized. So this does not solve our problem, though I can appreciate the fact that people at least recognize the problem.

How can we address this problem when the Bible declares that all people are born into sin? Even babies are sinners before a holy God-not because they have done something wrong, but because they have inherited Adam's sin.

The Bible says that all men are born into sin and shaped in inequity. When we are born, the Bible says, we are "children of wrath" (Ephesians 2:3). You don't have to teach a child how to lie, because the lies are already there. The child just needs the opportunity and the information.

David said, "Behold, I was brought forth in iniquity, and in sin my mother conceived me" (Psalm 51:5). You and I, just like David, were born sinners.

The Bible says that everyone is lost, including babies and infants. The Bible also says that all who are lost when they die will spend eternity separated from God. Now, here's where so many people encounter an emotional crisis, because babies and young children sometimes die. And sometimes people die without ever hearing the information of the Gospel.

In John 3, the fact that salvation is only by faith is made clear.

> Because if faith in Christ is necessary for salvation, then what happens to the huge group of people who cannot believe because they do not have the mental capacity to believe? And what happens to the huge group of people who can not believe because they do not have the information to believe?

"For God so loved the world, that He gave His only begotten Son, that whoever believes in Him shall not perish, but have eternal life. ... He who believes in Him is not judged; he who does not believe

has been judged already, because he has not believed in the name
of the only begotten Son of God."

John 3:16, 18

Now, verse 18 is a very important verse, because what it's saying is that belief is the opposite of rejection. So the question we must ask ourselves is, If belief in Christ is necessary for salvation, what happens to people who can't believe?

It's an important question because we know from the Bible that Jesus is the only way to salvation. He said in John 14:6, "I am the way, and the truth, and the life; no one comes to the Father but through Me." Acts 4:12 says, "And there is salvation in no one else; for there is no other name under heaven that has been given among men by which we must be saved."

> Because Jesus Christ said we must believe, the assumption is that believing is possible. God will never ask us to do something that we are incapable of doing, for that would be a trick.

The Bible clearly teaches that salvation comes only through belief and faith in Jesus Christ. He is the only way to heaven. All roads do not lead to glory; we get to heaven by going up a one-way highway through Jesus Christ. However, this only complicates our problem. Because if faith in Christ is necessary for salvation, then what happens to the huge group of people who cannot believe because they do not have the mental capacity to believe? And what happens to the huge group of people who cannot believe because they do not have the information to believe?

If God is good, then there must be an answer. We know that God *is* good, and we're about to discover that answer.

What concerns might a parent have after the death of a child? Why might that child's spiritual status be questioned?

_____

_____

_____

_____

_____

_____

_____

_____

_____

_____

_____

Read John 8:24; 11:25; and Romans 10:9-10, 13. What is a person to do to be saved?

_____

_____

_____

_____

_____

_____

_____

_____

_____

_____

_____

_____

2. THE PREMISE REGARDING THOSE WHO CAN'T BELIEVE

God has invited all people to respond to Him in faith. Now, that assumes something. It assumes that the ones He has invited have the capacity to respond.

> To have faith in Jesus Christ or to reject Jesus Christ, you must first have the ability to do one or the other. Or, to put it another way, God receives those who do believe because they can believe.

Because Jesus Christ said we must believe, the assumption is that believing is possible. God will never ask us to do something that we are incapable of doing, for that would be a trick. To ask a person to believe when that person cannot believe, and then to condemn that person for not believing, is double talk. It is confusion of the highest order.

There is no point in telling a newborn baby that he must believe in order to go to heaven when that child doesn't even know who his mother and father are. So, as we begin to answer the question, we must understand this premise: The command to believe is only applicable to those who can heed it.

The one who cannot believe is also the one who cannot reject. Do you understand what I'm saying? Those who do not have the capacity to believe also do not have the capacity to reject. If you can't say "yes" to Christ, then you also can't say "no."

This is why John 3:18 is so important in light of the problem we are examining. He said that we must believe, and that the ones who don't believe are the ones who reject.

John 3:36 says, "He who believes in the Son has eternal life; but he who does not obey the Son will not see life, but the wrath of God abides on him." You must be able to believe or be able to reject; otherwise, the command is pointless.

So our premise is this: To have faith in Jesus Christ or to reject Jesus Christ, you must first have the ability to do one or the other. Or, to put it another way, God receives those who do believe because they can believe.

Salvation is a free gift (Romans 3:24), and faith is just the link that receives the gift. Because salvation is a free gift by faith, anyone who exercises faith in the finished work of Jesus Christ gets the gift.

However, it does not hinder God from accomplishing salvation in those who can't believe. You see, faith is not a work to trust Christ; it is simply a condition of receiving to trust Christ. God would not be just if He held people accountable for that which they cannot do.

> Belief or lack of belief involves the will. It involves a choice. You can choose today to accept Christ, or you can choose today to reject Christ.

Now, in order to comprehend all of this, we must first understand that the decision to come to Christ for salvation is a decision that involves the will. Look at John 5:39-40:

> "You search the Scriptures because you think that in them you have eternal life; it is these that testify about Me· and you are unwilling to come to Me so that you may have life."

Please notice the word *unwilling*. Belief or lack of belief involves the will. It involves a choice. You can choose today to accept Christ, or you can choose today to reject Christ. Either way, you must make a choice. So faith only involves people with the capacity to make the choice.

Jesus said to the Jews,

> *"Jerusalem who kills the prophets and stones those who are sent to her! How often I wanted to gather your children together the way a hen gathers her chicks under her wings and you were unwilling."*
>
> *Matthew 23:37*

Every man who goes to hell has willed himself there. You must understand that. God allowed you to go there because you made the conscious decision not to place your eternal destiny in the hands of Jesus Christ alone.

To use the words of Abraham, "Shall not the Judge of all the earth deal justly?" (Genesis 18:25)

According to James 4:17 people who know the right thing to do, and then don't do it, are guilty of sin. Belief assumes knowledge and choice. Therefore, if you cannot know and therefore cannot choose, the condition of belief is not relevant to you. You cannot be expected to believe something that you are not aware of.

In school, the teachers only test you on what they taught you or what the book or resource was supposed to teach you. I was teaching a seminary class, and a student brought to my attention that I had asked a question on a test that I had never covered in class. In order to be fair and just, I re-scored all of the papers. If I was going to be fair, I could not condemn them for not knowing the answer to a question about something they had never heard before.

That was an example of my justice, but God's justice is much higher than mine. Or, to use the words of Abraham, "Shall not the Judge of all the earth deal justly?" Genesis 18:25. It would be wrong to condemn people for something which they could not do.

Now we have a premise, but we still have not solved our problem. God still cannot allow sin to enter into heaven. God cannot dwell with sin because He is pure. Yet we have a whole group of people who can't believe: the baby who died in a miscarriage, the child who was stillborn, the infant who died tragically, and the mentally retarded person who could not grasp the knowledge of God.

> God cannot allow sin to enter into heaven. God cannot dwell with sin because He is pure.

Many people would like to make an emotional argument and say, "Well, God will receive the babies because they were babies." That statement is not automatically true because God-who can never act out of character cannot just skip over their sin and allow them into heaven. He can't do that, His perfection won't allow it.

If God is good, then there must be an answer. We know that God *is* good, and we're about to discover that answer.

Read Genesis 18:25. How can understanding the character of God be helpful in dealing with the issue of those who cannot believe?

_____

_____

_____

_____

_____

Based on what you have seen, if a person is unable to believe, what else is that person able to do?

_____

_____

_____

_____

_____

_____

_____

3. THE PROVISION FOR THOSE WHO CAN'T BELIEVE

We have a problem and a premise. But, in order for the problem to be solved by the premise, God must first make a provision.

God has revealed Himself to us in two ways. The first way He has done this is through what is called general revelation. Romans 1 refers to this general revelation, describing it as the revelation of God that we have through nature. The world calls it Mother Nature, but it only exists because of Father God.

> "For the wrath of God is revealed from heaven against all ungodliness and unrighteousness of men who suppress the truth in unrighteousness; because that which is known about God is evident within them; for God made it evident to them. For since the creation of the world His invisible attributes; His eternal power and divine nature; have been clearly seen; being understood through what has been made; so that they are without excuse."
>
> _Romans 1:18-20_

So God has revealed Himself in two ways in creation. People say, "I can't see God." You don't have to see God-look at what He has done! If you go to a museum and see a painting by Rembrandt or some other magnificent work of art, you don't have to be a genius to know that each painting had to be painted by a painter.

It is assumed that if there is a painting, then there is a painter. Nobody in his right mind would assume a painting without a painter. But you don't need to know the painter to know this, and you don't need to see the painter to know this. Creation is God's masterpiece, and what a painting it is!

> It is assumed that if there is a painting, then there is a painter. Nobody in his right mind would assume a painting without a painter.

In the same way, you don't have to be a rocket scientist to know that if you have a watch, then that watch must have had a watchmaker. This is why evolution is the most foolish way of thinking you can come up with. To think that creation happened because of luck is like me taking apart my watch, removing all the little parts, throwing them all up into the air, and watching them all fall back into place, just as if I had never touched the watch. That will never happen, though, because you just don't get lucky and end up with a watch. Every watch has to have a designer.

When scientists tell you that the DNA has all the component parts to make the individual who he is-race, height, etc.-he is saying that human procreation is by design. Therefore, when those same scientists stand up in front of a classroom and tell the students that the world began with a big bang, they're talking nonsense.

This reminds me of the story of the guy who said, "I don't believe you Christians. I don't like Christianity. I don't like your God. And I don't like your holidays-the holidays where you worship God." The other guy said, "Well, you have a holiday." He said, "No, I don't." He said, "Yes, you do." He asked, "What is it?" He said, "April Fools' Day. Because the Bible says the fool has said in his heart, 'There is no God.'"

> When scientists tell you that the DNA has all the component parts to make the individual who he is—race, height, etc.—he is saying that human procreation is by design.

In fact, Romans 1:18 clearly shows us that men *suppress* the truth. They can understand it; they just don't want it. So they suppress it. Have you ever been to the beach and tried to lie down on a beach ball? You try to hold the ball under the water, but it just keeps trying to pop back up. But you keep trying to force it back down under the water. The Bible says that men don't have truth because they don't want it.

God's pictures are clearly seen, He says, by the things that were made. Psalm 19:1 says, "The heavens are telling of the glory of God; and their expanse is declaring the work of His hands."

God's creation is screaming out, "GOD!!" Verse 2 says, "Day to day pours forth speech, and night to night reveals knowledge"- which is precisely why we can even have science in the first place. Then the psalmist continues, "There is no speech, nor are there words; their voice is not heard. Their line has gone out through all the earth, and their utterances to the end of the world" (vv. 3-4).

God's voice is loud and clear, and men have to suppress it in order not to hear it. When you drive down the highway and see signs on the side of the road, those signs are there to guide you. But you don't see the signmaker; you just see the sign.

If the sign says "55 mph" and you're driving 75 miles per hour, chances are you'll get pulled over by a policeman. And when that happens, you can't say, "But, Officer, I never saw the signmaker, so I didn't know that I was supposed to pay attention to the sign." Guess what? You are without excuse.

Romans 1:20 says that because God's attributes are clearly seen, every one of us is without excuse. Man cannot say, "I didn't see God, so I didn't know that I was supposed to pay attention to the signs of nature." You cannot say that; the signs are clearly there. Therefore, men who go to hell are there because they have chosen to suppress, or hold down, what was evident in creation. Those who have suppressed the truth have seen it, ignored it, suppressed it, held it down, resisted it, and said "no" to It.

> God's creation is screaming out, "GOD!!!"

God never leaves Himself without a witness.

> *"In the generations gone by He permitted all the nations to go their own ways; and yet He did not leave Himself without witness in that He did good and gave you rains from heaven and fruitful seasons satisfying your hearts with food and gladness."*
>
> Acts 14:16-17

God always makes Himself absolutely clear, and we can see this in nature. This general revelation exists so that anyone who can look at creation is on the path to knowing God. The one who can look at creation may not know God personally or intimately, but he knows that God really does exist. Therefore, God's power is evident. Anyone who can paint a picture this big must be huge. The characteristics of God are seen in nature-especially His power and His wisdom.

This still does not solve our problem, though, because babies cannot understand nature. So now let's look at 1 Timothy 4:10: "For it is for this we labor and strive, because we have fixed our hope on the living God, who is the Savior of all men, especially of believers."

This verse says that God saves on two levels, not one. He saves all men *generically,* and He saves some men *particularly.* Those who are *particularly* saved are called believers; these people have the capacity to believe.

But in what way has God saved all men? The crux of the matter is this: The death of Jesus Christ removed the guilt of original sin for all people. Every baby born into the world is guilty of Adam's sin, for in Adam all die (I Corinthians 15:22).

All die because of Adam's sin, and God cannot overlook that. So He sent Jesus to die on the cross and remove the guilt of original sin. Because of Jesus' death on the cross, people no longer go to hell because of what Adam did; they now go to hell for what they do. They can no longer blame Adam, because God took care of Adam on the cross. Jesus paid for original sin.

> God always makes himself absolutely clear, and we can see this in nature. This general revelation exists so that anyone who can look at creation is on the path to knowing God.

This is why 2 Corinthians 5:18 says God reconciled the whole world to Himself. This is why Hebrews 2:9 says Jesus tasted death for every man. This is why John I:9 says that Jesus Christ, having come into the world, enlightens every man. The death of Jesus Christ addressed the problem of original sin.

A baby cannot believe or disbelieve, so the only thing that could send a baby to hell would be Adam's sin. But since the death of Jesus Christ took care of the problem of original sin, a baby that dies before reaching the age of accountability goes to heaven because the sin that would have taken him to hell was paid for by the death of Jesus on the cross.

> All die because of Adam's sin, and God cannot overlook that. So He sent Jesus to die on the cross and remove the guilt of original sin.

Babies do not go to heaven because God overlooked sin. Babies go to heaven because God dealt with sin on the cross when Jesus Christ became the Savior of all men.

Once a child reaches the age of accountability, however, he then sins by choice, not by chance. Once you reach the age where you understand the revelation of God, once you reach the age where you understand that God exists, once you reach the age where it is clear that you are a sinner, and once you reach the age where you can respond to the revelation of God, then the issue is no longer Adam's sin, but your own sin.

Everybody is born moving away from God, because everybody is born in sin. But until you reach the age of accountability, God allows the death of Jesus Christ to pick up the bill. But once you reach the age of accountability, you have to pay your own way. You have to make your own decisions about Jesus Christ, because now you are mentally capable of doing so and becoming a believer. At this point, you must make the choice to either accept or reject the revelation of God.

This raises another question, doesn't it? What if I am living in a foreign land and have never heard the name of Jesus Christ?

I would still be able to look up into the heavens and see that someone must be responsible for creation. Let's say that I acknowledge that someone. Let's say that I do not suppress the truth, hold down the truth, and resist the truth. In fact, I welcome it. I say, "Whoever You are out there, I don't know Your name, and I don't know much about You, but I know Someone must be responsible for all this. I welcome any knowledge."

The Bible says that any time anybody anywhere responds to the light that has been given to him, God will give him even more light. Always remember this: When a person with limited knowledge responds to what he *does* know, God then takes personal responsibility to provide that person with more information about Himself.

Now, this scenario raises yet another interesting question. Let's say you are living in some jungle somewhere. No missionary has ever come your way. You have never heard the name of Jesus. You know that Someone is responsible for creating all that you see around you, and you want to know Who that Someone is.

God can reach you one of three ways. First, He can send a missionary to say, "Let me tell you about the true God and how He became a man." This missionary would then present the Gospel to you.

> Everybody is born owing God, because everybody is born in sin. But until you reach the age of accountability, God allows the death of Jesus Christ to pick up the bill.

Second, God can supernaturally reveal Himself to you apart from a missionary. There have been missionaries who have gone to minister to tribes and told them about Jesus. And then people have said, "Oh, that's His name?"

God is all-powerful, and He can choose to supernaturally reveal Himself to those who seek Him.

> People in the Old Testament got saved, yet they had never heard the name of Jesus. He hadn't even been born yet. But those Old Testament saints were saved because they believed what God had revealed to them.

Third, God can choose to apply another dispensational category to them. Now, a dispensation is a certain way God works with a certain group of people based on the information He has given them. Everyone doesn't always have the whole story.

People in the Old Testament got saved, yet they had never heard the name of Jesus. He hadn't even been born yet. But these Old Testament saints were saved because they believed what God had revealed to them.

Abraham believed God (Genesis 15:6). Now, Abraham did not know anything about the name of Jesus at this time, but he believed what God told him. He believed what God had revealed to him. And in believing what God had revealed to him, the Bible says, Abraham was justified.

Am I saying that you can get saved without Jesus? No. Nobody can get saved without Jesus, because He's the Savior of all men. The babies who die have never heard His name, yet His death on the cross satisfied God as a payment for the guilt of all men. So, though a man can be saved without knowing Jesus' name, no man can be saved without Jesus.

Take a minute to step outside and just look around you. Observe the sky, the clouds, the trees, the grass, the flowers, or even the snow depending on where you are. In what ways can you see God's general revelation?

_____

_____

_____

_____

_____

_____

_____

_____

_____

Read Romans 1:18. On whom is God's wrath being revealed? What are these people doing?

_____

_____

_____

_____

_____

_____

_____

_____

_____

_____

_____

Read Jeremiah 29:13; Matthew 7:7-11; and Hebrews 6:11. What do God's promises say about His provision?

_____

_____

_____

_____

_____

_____

_____

_____

_____

4. THE PROOF REGARDING THOSE WHO CAN'T BELIEVE

Jesus Christ is the Savior of all men. He didn't die just to make men savable; He died to save from the consequences of original sin and from the consequences of personal sin. People do not go to hell for original sin; people go to hell for personal sin and for rejecting their Savior.

David's sin resulted in the death of his baby. Notice David's words in response to the death of his child:

> He said, "While the child was still alive I fasted and wept; for I said, who knows the LORD may be gracious to me that the child may live. But now he has died; why should I fast? Can I bring him back again? I will go to him but he will not return to me."
>
> 2 Samuel 12:22-23

> Though a man can be saved without knowing Jesus' name, no man can be saved without Jesus.

David understood that his child was going to be with God. Remember, he was going to live in the house of God forever. He knew he was going to heaven. David knew that he would go to be with his child, although his child could not come back and be with him.

Jesus Christ is the Savior of all men. He didn't die just to make men savable; He died to save men from the consequences of original sin and from the consequences of personal sin.

I have wonderful news for the mother who has lost an infant child: Your child was too young to understand the reality of God or the consequences of sin, and your child is in the presence of God today. Your child can't come back to you, but you can go to your child in the afterlife. You will see him or her again.

In fact, the parents who have lost young children are not only going to see their children in heaven, but they are going to see them as they were meant to be. They won't have any headaches, they won't be going through the teenage years, but they will be just as God created them to be.

Now, someone might ask how we can be sure that David wasn't just talking about death. What if David simply meant that he would be with his child in death? First, if death is all there is, then when you die-no matter how close your casket is laid next to them-you are not going to be *with* your children. The word *with* is a term of reunion; it's a term of fellowship.

Not only that, but look at what David did in verse 20: "So David arose from the ground, washed, anointed himself, and changed his clothes; and he came into the house of the LORD and worshiped." Well, what would have motivated David to worship if he didn't have hope? He worshiped because he knew he would be together with his son.

I want you to notice something else. Jesus said, "Truly I say to you, unless you are converted and become like children, you will not enter the kingdom of heaven" (Matthew 18:3). Unless we are converted and become like what? Children.

Why must we become like a child in order to be converted? Because we must become like a child to believe. In order to be converted, we must place ourselves in the hands of Jesus Christ. Mark says Jesus took the children into His arms (Mark 9:36).

To believe means to place your eternal destiny in the arms of Jesus Christ. And what do parents do? We pick the child up in our arms. Do you know what Jesus does? He picks the child up, too.

But when the child gets big, what does he do? He wants to do his own thing, and he wiggles right out of your arms. When you wiggle out of God's arms, you have reached the age of accountability. Before that time, you have been like a little child, who was covered, but now you must believe.

> I have wonderful news for the mother who has lost an infant child: You will see him or her again.

Jesus said in Matthew 18:10, "See that you do not despise one of these little ones, for I say to you that their angels in heaven continually see the face of My Father who is in heaven." What did He say? Children have angels.

But, in Hebrews 1:14, we learn that angels are "ministering spirits, sent out to render service for the sake of those who will inherit salvation." So the only people who have angels are believers.

> God wants you to be with Him in heaven. Satan wants you to be with him in hell. Satan divorced himself from God when he rebelled and was thrown out of heaven. Now they are both calling on you to live with them.

Now, reason with me. If the only people who have angels are believers, and children have angels, then, until they reach the age of accountability at which they can acknowledge their personal sin, they are under the protection of an angel. Who takes a child to heaven when he dies? An angel.

As you are reading this, you may have a tendency to say, "Well, if God has covered the children and will provide more light to those who respond to the initial light, then I don't have to witness. I don't have to preach the gospel."

If this is what you're thinking right now, you're wrong. The Bible tells us that men are suppressing the truth, and it is our responsibility to try to help pry them loose from that suppression. Maybe there is someone in your family who is trying to hold down the truth right now. You need to recognize that your family member is headed for hell, and you need to offer them the message of the Gospel, which is designed to open our eyes to the truth (Romans 1:16).

Satan is keeping so many people blinded to the truth of who God is, and he is also keeping them blinded to the fact that they must choose Christ. See, we cannot just sit around hoping that our friends and family will realize the truth. Men are faced with the reality of God, but Satan is so powerful and sin is so pleasurable that men are continuing to wear the blindfolds.

In Texas, we have a law that says when two parents get divorced, a child who is 12 years of age or older can decide where he wants to live. The mother and father are fighting over little Johnny, but the law treats Johnny as competent enough to express where he wants to live. And, because he understands the issues, he gets to make a choice.

God wants you to be with Him in heaven. Satan wants you to be with him in hell. Satan divorced himself from God when he rebelled and was thrown out of heaven. Now they are both calling on you to live with them.

My friend, where do you want to spend eternity? God has made every necessary provision for you to be able to choose the right place to live. He has paid everything necessary for you to choose Him. But if you do not choose Him, you are rejecting Him. And if you are rejecting Him, you're choosing Satan as your father and hell as your eternal home. Where are you planning to spend eternity?

Read Matthew 18:10 and Hebrews 1:14 again. What assurances do these verses offer?

_____

_____

_____

_____

_____

_____

_____

_____

_____

_____

What responsibility do you have to take God's Word and the Gospel of Jesus Christ to those who have never heard? Have these lessons "unburdend" you or motivated you?

_____

_____

_____

_____

_____

_____

_____

_____

_____

_____

_____

_____

> God has made every necessary provision for you to be able to choose the right place to live. He has paid everything necessary for you to choose Him.

How can God be fair when so many tribes and peoples have never seen a missionary, and when so many have never seen one Gospel presentation over a television or a radio?

God is fair because He has already taken care of everyone—even the children, even the mentally incompetent, even those who have never heard.

Our God is not a monster who schemes against us above the clouds. He never compromises His justice, and He takes no pleasure in the destruction of the wicked.

But, my friend, don't confuse the love of God to the point that you miss the holiness of God, the righteousness of God, the justice of God, and the wrath of God.

One thing God can never tolerate is the one who rejects Him after He has gone to such great lengths to reveal Himself to us.

It would be rare to find an American with an excuse, because not only do we have nature to look at, but we have education of all sorts coming from our churches, our bookstores, our libraries, our TV programs, our radio programs, and people who are not afraid to share their faith.

God has taken care of all those who can't believe. But you can believe, my friend. Have you believed in God, and have you called upon the name of Lord Jesus Christ?

The afterlife is real, and your eternal destiny is up to you. Are you satisfied with the choice you've made? If not, there's still time to change your mind.